REVISE EDEXCEL GCSE (9–1)

English Language

REVISION WORKBOOK

Series Consultant: Harry Smith

Authors: Julie Hughes and David Grant

Reviewer: Esther Menon

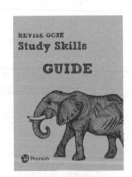

Contents

1-to-1 page match with the Revision Guide ISBN 9781447988083

A small bit of small print
Edexcel publishes Sample Assessment Material and the Specification on its website. This is the official content and this book should be used in conjunction with it. The questions in this book have been written to help you practise what you have learned in your revision. Remember: the real exam questions may not look like this.

Planning your exam time

It is important to use your time wisely in the exam. Look closely at the examples of exam-style questions below. **You don't need to answer these questions**. Instead, look at the marks and think about how long you should spend answering each type of question.

The total time allowed here is for Section A – Reading and Section B – Writing. The questions below are examples of those you might find in Section A – Reading.

Paper 1

Time allowed: 1 hour and 45 minutes

1 From lines 1–3, identify the phrase which explains why the narrator is content with his situation. **(1 mark)**

3 In lines 8–15, how does the writer use language and structure to suggest that the room is unwelcoming?
Support your views with reference to the text. **(6 marks)**

The total time allowed here is for Section A – Reading and Section B – Writing. The questions below are examples of those you might find in Section A – Reading.

Paper 2

Time allowed: 2 hours

1 In lines 1–10, identify **two** reasons why the writer feels the experience he is about to face should be easy. **(2 marks)**

6 John F Kennedy attempts to engage his audience through the descriptions of man's achievements through time.
Evaluate how successfully this is achieved.
Support your answer with detailed reference to the text. **(15 marks)**

7 (a) The two texts are both about advances in technology.
What similarities are there in what they say about these advances?
Use evidence from both texts to support your answer. **(6 marks)**

1 How many minutes should you spend reading the source texts and questions before you start each exam? ....

2 How many minutes should you spend on Paper 1, Question 1? ....

3 What part of the extract should you refer to in your answer to Paper 1, Question 3?

....

4 How many minutes should you spend on Paper 2, Question 6?

....

5 How many texts should you use to answer Paper 2, Question 7 (a)?

....

6 Which of the following should you do before you start to answer any of the questions? Circle your choices.

- Read all the questions.
- Skim read the source texts to identify the main ideas and themes.
- Highlight or annotate relevant information in the texts.
- Read the texts a second time.
- Notice how many marks are awarded per question and work out how much time to spend on each question.

Reading texts explained

Read this short extract from *The Woman in White*, then answer Question 1 below. Part (a) has been done for you.

> The gleams and flashes of the light showed me the servant's face staring up vacantly under the wall – the clerk risen to his feet on the tombstone, wringing his hands in despair – and the scanty population of the village, haggard men and terrified women, clustered beyond in the churchyard – all appearing and disappearing, in the red of the dreadful glare, in the black of the choking smoke.

Guided

1 (a) Highlight or underline any words or phrases you think create atmosphere.

(b) What type of atmosphere do you think is created here?

. . . .

. . . .

. . . .

. . . .

. . . .

. . . .

. . . .

. . . .

> Read as much and as widely as you can outside lesson time. This will help you start to think about how writers create atmosphere and character.

Now read this short extract from *Bad Blood*, then answer Question 2 below.

21st

> The only way to win at this game was to approach very slowly and see if you could spot your town in time, but since most kids couldn't read very well (or at all) this didn't help a lot. I did all right with something beginning with B (Bolton or Blackburn or Birkenhead or Birmingham) but I cried anyway, I always did. Although we may not have found out much about geography that day, we were being taught a lesson, the usual one: to know our place. Hanmer wasn't on the map and Hanmer was where we were. Most of us, according to Mr Palmer, would be muck-shovellers.

2 (a) Highlight or underline any words or phrases that suggest the narrator's school years were hard.

(b) Use your evidence to comment on the writer's point of view about her school years.

. . . .

. . . .

. . . .

. . . .

. . . .

. . . .

. . . .

Reading questions explained 1

There are four assessment objectives in Section A Reading: Assessment objective 1 (AO1), Assessment objective 2 (AO2), Assessment objective 3 (AO3) and Assessment objective 4 (AO4). Read AO1 and AO2 below.

Assessment objective 1

(a) Identify and interpret explicit and implicit information and ideas

(b) Select and synthesise evidence from different texts

Assessment objective 2

Explain, comment on and analyse how writers use language and structure to achieve effects and influence readers, using relevant subject terminology to support their views

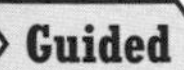

Guided

1 Look at the following exam-style questions. **You don't need to answer these questions.** Instead, identify the assessment objective (or the part of the assessment objective) that is being tested and circle it.

Paper 1

1 From lines 4–7, identify the phrase which explains why the narrator is frightened to tell his uncle of his engagement. **(1 mark)**

(a) The question above tests:  AO1(a) AO1(b) AO2

Paper 1

2 From lines 1–5, give **two** reasons why the narrator is unhappy in his uncle's house. You may use your own words or quotation from the text. **(2 marks)**

(b) The question above tests: AO1(a) AO1(b) AO2

Paper 2

2 Give **one** example from lines 1–15 of how the writer uses language to show how badly behaved teenagers can be. Support your example with a detailed text reference. **(2 marks)**

(c) The question above tests: AO1(a) AO1(b) AO2

Paper 2

4 How many modes will be on offer when Goldwasser's product first goes on the market? **(1 mark)**

(d) The question above tests: AO1(a) AO1(b) AO2

Paper 2

7 (a) The two texts are about school life. In what ways are the children and teachers in the texts similar? Use evidence from both texts to support your answer. **(6 marks)**

(e) The question above tests: AO1(a) AO1(b) AO2

Had a go ☐ Nearly there ☐ Nailed it! ☐

Reading questions explained 2

Read AO3 and AO4 below.

Assessment objective 3
Compare writers' ideas and perspectives, as well as how these are conveyed, across two or more texts

Assessment objective 4
Evaluate texts critically and support this with appropriate textual references

1 Look at the following exam-style questions. **You don't need to answer them.** Instead, identify the assessment objective that is being tested and circle it.

Paper 1

4 In this extract, there is an attempt to create tension.
Evaluate how successfully this is achieved.
Support your views with detailed reference to the text. **(15 marks)**

(a) The question above tests: AO3 (AO4)

Paper 2

6 Clive James attempts to entertain the reader through the descriptions of his boyhood exploits.
Evaluate how successfully this is achieved.
Support your views with detailed reference to the text. **(15 marks)**

(b) The question above tests: AO3 AO4

7 **(b)** Compare how the writers of 'OK, you try teaching 13-year-olds' and *Bad Blood* present their ideas and perspectives about education.
Support your answer with detailed reference to the texts. **(14 marks)**

(c) The question above tests: AO3 AO4

2 Look back at the exam-style questions on page 3. Put a tick next to the questions that tell you which lines you should focus on in your answer.

3 If no line numbers are given in the question, how much of the extract text should you use for your answer?

....

Reading the questions

Read the exam-style question below. **You don't need to answer this question**. Instead, think about what it is asking you to do, then answer the questions that follow.

Paper 1

> 2 From lines 6–11 give **two** reasons why it is not possible to follow Eustacia.
> You may use your own words or quotations from the text. **(2 marks)**

Guided

1 (a) Highlight or underline:
- the part of the extract you are being asked to use for your answer
- how many pieces of information you are being asked to find
- the focus of the question.

It is very important to read the questions carefully so that you know which part of the extract to use in your answer.

(b) Which word in exam-style Question 2 above shows that you only need to **find** the reasons, rather than give a full explanation for each one?

....

2 Look at the exam-style questions below. **You don't need to answer these questions**. Instead, annotate each question to show the following information:
- how many texts you need to write about
- how much of each text you should use for your answer
- the key words in the question
- how long you should spend on your answer.

Paper 1

> 3 In lines 7–12, how does the writer use language and structure to show the change in the weather?
> Support your views with reference to the text. **(6 marks)**

Paper 2

> 6 Lorna Sage attempts to make the reader feel that she had a harsh education in order to gain sympathy.
> Evaluate how successfully this is achieved.
> Support your views with detailed reference to the text. **(15 marks)**

Paper 2

> 7 **(a)** The two texts describe the way mothers worry about their children taking risks.
> What similarities are there between the risks taken by the children in the texts?
> Use evidence from both texts to support your answer. **(6 marks)**

Had a go ☐ Nearly there ☐ Nailed it! ☐

Skimming for the main idea or theme

Read the following extract from 'OK, you try teaching 13-year-olds', then answer the questions below.

21st

> Shocking news: a young trainee languages teacher on placement at Tarleton High in Lancashire "lost it" in class, barricaded the door with furniture, trapping the pupils, and threatened to kill them with something nasty that she had in her handbag.

Guided

1 (a) What does the headline suggest about the main idea or theme of the article?

The headline suggests that the main idea of the article will be the difficulties faced by teachers.

(b) What does the opening sentence suggest about the main idea or theme of the article?

The opening sentence suggests that the main idea will be the difficulties of teaching, although it also suggests ....

....

....

Now read these sentences from the end of the same article, then answer the questions below.

> Her career is now ruined. But the children were "petrified … burst into tears" and were offered "support". The pathetic little wets. She was pretending, you fools – dredging up a last desperate ploy to shut the monsters up. If she had cried, they would have laughed out loud. Hopefully, she won't be sacked. If that's what she really, really wants.

2 What does the end of the article suggest about the article's main idea or theme?

....

....

3 Do the ideas expressed at the end of the article differ from those you found at the beginning?

....

....

> Skim reading a text can give you a good idea of what it is about before you read it more closely. Look at:
> - the headline, title or headings
> - the first sentence of each paragraph
> - the last sentence of the text.

Turn to the full article, 'OK, you try teaching 13-year-olds', on page 101.
Skim read it for 30 seconds, then answer Question 4.

4 In one sentence, sum up the main idea in the article as a whole.

....

....

....

Annotating the texts

Read this extract from *The Poor Relation's Story*. It has been annotated by a student.

It was a large room with a small fire, and there was a great bay window in it which the rain had marked in the night as if with the tears of houseless people. It stared upon a raw yard, with a cracked stone pavement, and some rusted iron railings half uprooted, whence an ugly out-building that had once been a dissecting-room (in the time of the great surgeon who had mortgaged the house to my uncle), stared at it.

We rose so early always, that at that time of the year we breakfasted by candle-light. When I went into the room, my uncle was so contracted by the cold and so huddled together in his chair behind the one dim candle, that I did not see him until I was close to the table.

A Contrast between 'large' room and 'small' fire suggests it is cold

B Simile – 'tears' suggests sadness, 'houseless' suggests neglect and poverty

C Adjective 'raw' suggests rough and unprotected

D Negative adjectives build a picture of neglect and decay

E References to the cold, dark, early mornings suggest discomfort

Now read this exam-style question. **You don't need to answer it**. Instead, think about what it is asking you to do, then answer the questions that follow.

Paper 1

3 In lines 11–15, how does the writer use language and structure to make the setting seem unwelcoming?
Support your views with reference to the text. **(6 marks)**

1 Which of the annotations A to E above would help you to answer this exam-style question? Circle your choices (two have been selected for you).

2 Which annotated detail above won't help you to answer the exam-style question? Explain your choice.

....

....

Now read the rest of the extract from *The Poor Relation's Story* on page 98, then answer Question 3.

3 Annotate the extract from *The Poor Relation's Story* on page 98, identifying any words or phrases that would help you to answer the exam-style question below. **You don't need to answer the exam-style question itself**.

Paper 1

4 In this extract, there is an attempt to create sympathy for the narrator.
Evaluate how successfully this is achieved.
Support your views with detailed reference to the text. **(15 marks)**

When you are annotating, don't just identify the technique. Make a note of the effect on the reader.

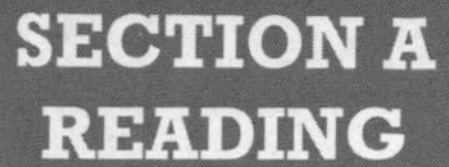

Putting it into practice

Read the full extract from *The Return of the Native* on page 96, then answer Questions 1 and 2.

1 (a) Highlight, circle or underline any words or phrases in the extract from *The Return of the Native* that would help you to answer the exam-style question below. You don't need to answer the exam-style question itself.

Paper 1

3 In lines 22–27, how does the writer use language and structure to suggest that Eustacia might be running away to danger?
Support your views with reference to the text. **(6 marks)**

(b) Make notes about the effect that each word or phrase you have identified has on the reader.

2 Now use your annotations and notes from Question 1 to write the first two paragraphs of an answer to the exam-style Question 3.

When you tackle this kind of question in the exam, remember to:
- spend about 12 minutes on your answer
- highlight key words in the question so that you get the focus right
- use only the lines of the text referred to in the question.

Remember: You are only being asked to write part of an answer on this page. In the exam, you will be given more space to write a full answer.

Putting it into practice

Read the full extract from *Unreliable Memoirs* on page 104, then answer Questions 1 and 2.

1 (a) Highlight, circle or underline any words or phrases in the extract from *Unreliable Memoirs* that would help you to answer the exam-style question below. You don't need to answer the exam-style question itself.

Paper 2

> **6** Clive James attempts to entertain the reader through the descriptions of his boyhood exploits.
> Evaluate how successfully this is achieved.
> Support your views with detailed reference to the text. **(15 marks)**

(b) Make notes about the effect that each word or phrase you have identified has on the reader.

....

....

....

....

....

....

2 Now use your annotations and notes from Question 1 to write the first two paragraphs of an answer to the exam-style Question 6.

When you tackle this kind of question in the exam, remember to:
- spend about 15 minutes on your answer
- highlight key words in the question so that you get the focus right
- focus on the way the ideas and point of view are expressed by the writer.

....

....

....

....

....

....

....

....

....

....

....

....

....

....

Remember: You are only being asked to write part of an answer on this page. In the exam, you will be given more space to write a full answer.

Had a go ☐ Nearly there ☐ Nailed it! ☐

Explicit information and ideas

Skim read the full extract from 'We choose to go to the moon' on page 102, then look at the exam-style question below. **You don't need to answer this question**. Instead, think about what it is asking you to do, then answer the questions that follow.

Paper 2

4 How many new inventions became available the month before the speech? **(1 mark)**

1 Circle the most effective style of answer for the exam-style question above.

4 inventions became available

electric lights and telephones and automobiles and airplanes

Four

2 Explain why the style you have chosen is the most effective way to answer the question.

....

....

3 Read the full extract from *The Poor Relation's Story* on page 98. Then answer the exam-style question below.

Paper 1

1 From lines 1–3, identify the phrase which explains why the narrator is happy even though his life at his uncle's house is uncomfortable. **(1 mark)**

....

4 Now read the full extract from 'OK, you try teaching 13-year-olds' on page 101. Then answer the exam-style questions below.

Paper 2

1 In lines 30–34, identify **two** things a teacher must be. **(2 marks)**

....

....

Paper 2

4 At which school was the young teacher working on placement? **(1 mark)**

....

For this type of question, keep your answers as short as possible. Don't copy whole sentences from the extract.

Implicit ideas

Read this short extract from *The Poor Relation's Story*.

My life at my uncle Chill's was of a spare dull kind, and my garret chamber was as dull, and bare, and cold, as an upper prison room in some stern northern fortress. But, having Christiana's love, I wanted nothing upon earth. I would not have changed my lot with any human being.

Avarice was, unhappily, my uncle Chill's master-vice. Though he was rich, he pinched, and scraped, and clutched, and lived miserably. As Christiana had no fortune, I was for some time a little fearful of confessing our engagement to him; but, at length I wrote him a letter, saying how it all truly was. I put it into his hand one night, on going to bed.

Now look at this exam-style question relating to the text extract. **You don't need to answer it**. Instead, answer Question 1 below.

Paper 1

2 From lines 1–7, give **two** reasons why the narrator was unhappy at his uncle's house. You may use your own words or quotations from the text. **(2 marks)**

To identify implicit ideas you need to read between the lines and think about what the writer is suggesting or implying. Explicit ideas are not hidden – you just need to find short quotations or paraphrase what is already in the text.

Guided

1 Any two of these points could be used to answer the question. For each point, decide whether the information is explicit or implicit. Some have been done for you.

Life was dull.	(Explicit) / Implicit
His room is cold.	Explicit / Implicit
He feels trapped.	Explicit / Implicit
His uncle is mean.	Explicit / Implicit
He is scared of his uncle.	Explicit / (Implicit)

Now read this extract from *The Woman in White*, then answer Question 2.

I looked round at my two companions. The servant had risen to his feet – he had taken the lantern, and was holding it up vacantly at the door. Terror seemed to have struck him with downright idiocy – he waited at my heels, he followed me about when I moved like a dog. The clerk sat crouched up on one of the tombstones, shivering, and moaning to himself. The one moment in which I looked at them was enough to show me that they were both helpless.

Hardly knowing what I did, acting desperately on the first impulse that occurred to me, I seized the servant and pushed him against the vestry wall.

2 Find four **implicit** ideas in the extract above that suggest the servant is scared.

(a) ....

(b) ....

(c) ....

(d) ....

Short questions on explicit and implicit information are only worth one mark for each point you make, so keep your answers brief. You don't always need to use quotations – you can also use your own words.

Had a go ☐ Nearly there ☐ Nailed it! ☐

Inference

Read this short extract from *The Return of the Native*, then answer Questions 1 and 2 below.

A sudden recollection had flashed on her this moment – she had not money enough for undertaking a long journey. Amid the fluctuating sentiments of the day her unpractical mind had not dwelt on the necessity of being well-provided, and now that she thoroughly realized the conditions she sighed bitterly and ceased to stand erect, gradually crouching down under the umbrella as if she were drawn into the Barrow by a hand from beneath.

1 Highlight or underline any phrases in the extract above that suggest Eustacia has not prepared properly for her journey.

Guided

2 What impression of Eustacia do you get from this short extract? Include two points, and use a short quotation to support each point and back up your answer.

When answering a question like this, think about what is suggested or implied about a character by their actions (or those of others) in the scene.

(a) The extract suggests that Eustacia ....

....

....

(b) ....

....

Now read this short extract, also from *The Woman in White*, then answer Question 3 below.

Hardly knowing what I did, acting desperately on the first impulse that occurred to me, I seized the servant and pushed him against the vestry wall. "Stoop!" I said, "and hold by the stones. I am going to climb over you to the roof – I am going to break the skylight, and give him some air!"

The man trembled from head to foot, but he held firm. I got on his back, with my cudgel in my mouth, seized the parapet with both hands, and was instantly on the roof. In the frantic hurry and agitation of the moment, it never struck me that I might let out the flame instead of letting in the air.

Guided

3 Write about your impressions of the narrator.

The narrator is presented as capable of making decisions quickly and instinctively under pressure, as he acts 'desperately' on his 'first impulse' rather than stopping to think. The words 'seized' and 'pushed' suggest ....

....

....

....

....

....

....

....

....

....

....

Interpreting information and ideas

Read this short extract from 'Dear daughter', then answer Question 1.

You're 15 now and maturing into an intelligent, independent young lady – and I am proud to call you my daughter. But like all young people today, you're susceptible to the pressures and pitfalls of the pacey technological age we live in. What am I on about? Social media.

Back in the dark ages, when I was a teenager, the only way I could get hold of my friends when I was back home after school was the telephone…

Please think before you press 'send' on a provocative image. Think about who will see it and what it says about you…

Guided

1 Look at the words and phrases that have been underlined in the extract above and explain their meaning in your own words. The first two have been done for you.

(a) 'susceptible to' Easily influenced by

(b) 'pitfalls' Hidden dangers or traps

(c) 'pacey' ....

(d) 'the dark ages' ....

(e) 'provocative'. ....

> Try reading the text before and after the word or phrase you need to explain. This may help you to infer the meaning. Remember that words and phrases can mean different things depending on the topic of the whole text.

Now read this short extract from *The Poor Relation's Story*, then answer Question 2.

My life at my uncle Chill's was of a spare dull kind, and my garret chamber was as dull, and bare, and cold, as an upper prison room in some stern northern fortress.

2 (a) In what part of his uncle's house is the narrator's room? ....

(b) Explain how you can tell this from the extract. Aim to include a comment on the word 'garret'.

....

....

....

Now read this short extract, also from *The Poor Relation's Story*, then answer Question 3.

Betsy Snap was a withered, hard-favoured, yellow old woman – our only domestic – always employed at this time of the morning, in rubbing my uncle's legs. As my uncle adjured her to look at me, he put his lean grip on the crown of her head, she kneeling beside him, and turned her face towards me.

3 How do the underlined words in the extract above help to describe Betsy Snap's position in the household?

(a) domestic. ....

....

(b) adjured. ....

....

Had a go ☐ Nearly there ☐ Nailed it! ☐

Using evidence

Read this short extract from 'We choose to go to the moon', then answer Question 1.

> We mean to be a part of it – we mean to lead it. For the eyes of the world now look into space, to the moon and to the planets beyond, and we have vowed that we shall not see it governed by a hostile flag of conquest, but by a banner of freedom and peace. We have vowed that we shall not see space filled with weapons of mass destruction, but with instruments of knowledge and understanding.

Guided

1 Use the short quotations underlined in the extract above to explain the writer's feelings about space travel.

The writer obviously feels very strongly about space travel as he wants America to 'lead' the race to space. He feels it is a global issue as the 'eyes of the world' are on it, and his use of the word 'vowed' suggests he ....

....

....

....

....

Now read this short extract, also from 'We choose to go to the moon', then answer Question 2.

> Whether it will become a force for good or ill depends on man, and only if the United States occupies a position of pre-eminence can we help decide whether this new ocean will be a sea of peace or a new terrifying theater of war. I do not say that we should or will go unprotected against the hostile misuse of space any more than we go unprotected against the hostile use of land or sea, but I do say that space can be explored and mastered without feeding the fires of war, without repeating the mistakes that man has made in extending his writ around this globe of ours.

Paraphrasing can be a useful way to support your points when you are evaluating a text as a whole. However, remember to use short quotations when you are analysing language.

Guided

2 Complete the following explanation by paraphrasing the information in the short extract above.

The writer feels that it is up to man to determine whether ....

....

....

....

When using quotations, remember that:
- short quotations are most effective
- you must use quotations rather than paraphrasing when explaining the effects of language
- all quotations must be in quotation marks and copied correctly from the text.

3 Which of the following should you do when using a longer quotation? Circle your choice(s).

(a) Introduce it with a colon.

(b) Include it as part of your sentence.

(c) Start the quotation on a new line.

(d) Put the quotation in quotation marks.

Point – Evidence – Explain

Read this short extract from 'OK, you try teaching 13-year-olds', then answer the questions that follow.

Shocking news: a young trainee languages teacher on placement at Tarleton High in Lancashire "lost it" in class, barricaded the door with furniture, trapping the pupils, and threatened to kill them with something nasty that she had in her handbag. But why shocking? Imagine yourself in her place, "teaching" about 30 13- or 14-year-old creatures. Do you have one or two in your house? Are they polite, quiet and cooperative? Or are they breathtakingly insolent, noisy, crabby, offensive, skulking, smoking, drugging, and whingeing that they are not suitably entertained? What if you had 30? Wouldn't you like something in your handbag to shut the little toads up?

1 The point below could be used to comment on the writer's use of language and its effect on the reader. Which piece of evidence below (A or B) most effectively supports this point? Circle your choice.

Point: The writer uses lists of adjectives to emphasise how difficult it can be to deal with teenagers.

Evidence A: 'whingeing that they are not suitably entertained'

Evidence B: 'insolent, noisy, crabby, offensive, ...'

2 Explain why the evidence you have chosen is the most effective for supporting the above point.

....

....

Guided

3 Select effective evidence from the extract to support the point below. Then choose the most effective explanation from the options given. Circle your choice.

Point: The writer uses strong verbs to emphasise the shocking nature of the teacher's actions.

Evidence: For example, she uses the words ....

....

Explanation A: These verbs emphasise how badly the teacher treated the children.

Explanation B: These verbs suggest that the teacher treated the children like prisoners. They also give the impression that she had completely lost her ability to manage the class and that she literally wanted to cause them harm.

4 Write one or two sentences, describing why your choice of explanation is more effective.

....

....

Point-Evidence-Explain, or P-E-E, is particularly useful if you are asked to comment on language and structure, or to evaluate or compare a text. Improve your P-E-E paragraphs by using more than one piece of evidence to support a fully developed point.

Had a go ☐ Nearly there ☐ Nailed it! ☐

Putting it into practice

Read the full extract from *Shirley* on page 97, then answer the exam-style questions below.

Paper 1

1 From lines 1–7, identify the phrase that suggests Malone is not interested in nature. **(1 mark)**

....

Paper 1

2 From lines 7–12, give **two** examples of how the sky is described to show the weather is stormy. **(2 marks)**

....

....

Now write two P-E-E paragraphs of an answer to the exam-style question below.

When you tackle this kind of question in the exam, remember to:

- spend about 12 minutes on your answer
- identify the main focus of the question
- read the text carefully and annotate it with your ideas
- only use the lines of the extract referred to in the question.

Paper 1

3 In lines 25–30, how does the writer use language and structure to create a change in atmosphere? Support your views with reference to the text. **(6 marks)**

....

....

....

....

....

....

....

....

....

....

....

....

....

....

....

....

Remember: You are only being asked to write part of an answer on this page. In the exam, you will be given more space to write a full answer.

Putting it into practice

Read the full extract from 'OK, you try teaching 13-year-olds' on page 101. Then write three P-E-E paragraphs of an answer to the exam-style question below.

When you tackle this kind of question in the exam, remember to:

- spend about 15 minutes on your answer
- read the question carefully and highlight the main focus
- read the text carefully and annotate it with your ideas
- refer to the whole text as no line numbers are given
- comment on how the writer uses language and structure and what the effects are on the reader.

Paper 2

3 Analyse how the writer uses language and structure to interest and engage readers. Support your views with detailed reference to the text. **(15 marks)**

Remember: You are only being asked to write part of an answer on this page. In the exam, you will be given more space to write a full answer.

Had a go ☐ Nearly there ☐ Nailed it! ☐

Word classes

Read this short extract from 'OK, you try teaching 13-year-olds', then answer Questions 1 and 2.

Shocking news: a young trainee languages teacher on placement at Tarleton High in Lancashire "lost it" in class, barricaded the door with furniture, trapping the pupils, and threatened to kill them with something nasty that she had in her handbag. But why shocking? Imagine yourself in her place, "teaching" about 30 13- or 14-year-old creatures. Do you have one or two in your house? Are they polite, quiet and cooperative? Or are they breathtakingly insolent, noisy, crabby, offensive, skulking, smoking, drugging, and whingeing that they are not suitably entertained?

Verb

Adverb

Guided

1 Circle and label at least one example of each of the following word classes. Two have been done for you:

- noun
- verb
- adverb
- adjective.

Remember that adjectives can become comparatives (e.g. noisier, more insolent) and superlatives (e.g. noisiest, most insolent).

2 The writer uses lists of adjectives in her rhetorical questions about teenagers. What effect do these lists of adjectives have on the reader?

....

....

....

Now read this short extract from *Shirley*, then answer Question 3.

He did not, therefore, care to contrast the sky as it now appeared – a muffled, streaming vault, all black, save where, towards the east, the furnaces of Stilbro' ironworks threw a tremulous lurid shimmer on the horizon – with the same sky on an unclouded frosty night. He did not trouble himself to ask where the constellations and the planets were gone, or to regret the "black-blue" serenity of the air-ocean which those white islets stud, and which another ocean, of heavier and denser element, now rolled below and concealed.

3 In this extract, the writer uses adjectives and verbs to describe the setting. Identify two examples of each and explain their effects on the reader.

(a) Adjective ....

....

(b) Adjective ....

....

(c) Verb ....

....

(d) Verb ....

....

Connotations

Read this short extract from 'We choose to go to the moon', then answer Question 1.

> Those who came before us made certain that this country rode the first (waves) of the industrial revolutions, the first waves of modern invention, and the first wave of nuclear power, and this generation does not intend to founder in the (backwash) of the coming age of space. We mean to be a part of it – we mean to lead it. For the eyes of the world now look into space, to the moon and to the planets beyond, and we have vowed that we shall not see it governed by a hostile flag of conquest, but by a (banner) of freedom and peace. We have vowed that we shall not see space filled with weapons of mass destruction, but with (instruments) of knowledge and understanding.

1 (a) Draw lines to match the circled words or phrases to their possible connotations.

(waves)	sign of protest
	symbol of celebration
(backwash)	receding
	waste water going backwards
(banner)	measuring devices
	professional tools
(instruments)	something that cannot be stopped

> Words can have different meanings depending on their context – what comes before and after them in a text. Thinking about the context of a word will help you to understand its connotations.

(b) What ideas and attitudes about the space race do the circled words or phrases suggest to the reader?

....

....

....

....

Now read this short extract (lines 34–38) from *Shirley*, then answer Question 2.

> He came to a little white house – you could see it was white even through this dense darkness – and knocked at the door. A fresh-faced servant opened it. By the candle she held was revealed a narrow passage, terminating in a narrow stair. Two doors covered with crimson baize, a strip of crimson carpet down the steps, contrasted with light-coloured walls and white floor, made the little interior look clean and fresh.

2 Circle two words or phrases from the extract above that create atmosphere. Write a sentence commenting on the connotations of each one.

(a) ....

....

(b) ....

....

Had a go ☐ Nearly there ☐ Nailed it! ☐

Figurative language

Read this short extract from *The Return of the Native*, then answer Question 1.

The gloom of the night was funereal; all nature seemed clothed in crape. The spiky points of the fir trees behind the house rose into the sky like the turrets and pinnacles of an abbey. Nothing below the horizon was visible save a light which was still burning in the cottage of Susan Nunsuch.

Guided

1 What does the simile 'like the turrets and pinnacles of an abbey' suggest about the night Eustacia runs away from home?

The writer uses the simile 'like the turrets and pinnacles of an abbey', which has connotations of ....

....

This suggests to the reader ....

....

Now read this short extract from *The Woman in White*, then answer Question 2.

19th

I struck at the skylight, and battered in the cracked, loosened glass at a blow. The fire leaped out like a wild beast from its lair. If the wind had not chanced, in the position I occupied, to set it away from me, my exertions might have ended then and there.

2 Identify one simile from the extract above. Write one or two sentences commenting on why the writer has used it and its effect on the reader.

....

....

....

Now read this short extract from *Shirley*, then answer Question 3.

19th

He could walk miles on the most varying April day and never see the beautiful dallying of earth and heaven – never mark when a sunbeam kissed the hill-tops, making them smile clear in green light, or when a shower wept over them, hiding their crests with the low-hanging, dishevelled tresses of a cloud. He did not, therefore, care to contrast the sky as it now appeared – a muffled, streaming vault, all black, save where, towards the east, the furnaces of Stilbro' ironworks threw a tremulous lurid shimmer on the horizon – with the same sky on an unclouded frosty night.

Don't just identify and name a figurative device used in a text. Remember to comment on the effect the device has on the reader.

3 Identify where the writer has used personification in the extract above. Write one or two sentences commenting on why the writer has used it and its effect on the reader.

....

....

....

LEARNING OBJECTIVES

This lesson will help you to:

- understand and analyse how writers introduce and develop fictional characters in their writing
- understand how writers develop and use setting and atmosphere.

CHARACTER, ATMOSPHERE AND EMOTION

Understanding character is not easy. Good writers subtly reveal aspects of a character's personality through a combination of description, behaviour and dialogue.

ACTIVITY 1

SKILLS CREATIVITY, COMMUNICATION

▼ WHAT'S IN YOUR POCKET?

The best way to approach character is to understand how characters are created, to put yourself in someone else's shoes or, in this case, pocket!

Create an imaginary character. Think of a few details about them such as name, age and job. Now imagine which objects they might carry in their pocket or bag. Write down or draw at least three of these and put them into an envelope. You have now created your character's 'pocket' or 'bag'.

Swap envelopes with a partner. Remove the items from your partner's envelope, one item at a time. Try to imagine what kind of person would own these items. Share your ideas with your partner.

Write a short paragraph about the character your partner created, using some of the items in their 'pocket' to develop the character.

CHARACTER IN NOVELS

INTRODUCING A CHARACTER

It is often said that first impressions are the most important, and this is often true of fictional characters. The following extract from Bram Stoker's novel *Dracula* introduces the iconic titular character.

▼ FROM *DRACULA* BY BRAM STOKER

Within, stood a tall old man, clean shaven save for a long white moustache, and clad in black from head to foot, without a single speck of colour about him anywhere. He held in his hand an antique silver lamp, in which the flame burned without a chimney or globe of any kind, throwing long quivering shadows as it flickered in the draught of the Dracula open door. The old man motioned me in with his right hand with a courtly gesture, saying in excellent English, but with a strange intonation.

'Welcome to my house! Enter freely and of your own free will!' He made no motion of stepping to meet me, but stood like a statue, as though his gesture of welcome had fixed him into stone. The instant, however, that I had stepped over the threshold, he moved impulsively forward, and holding out his hand grasped mine with a strength which made me wince, an effect which was not lessened by the fact that it seemed cold as ice, more like the hand of a dead than a living man. Again he said.

'Welcome to my house! Enter freely. Go safely, and leave something of the happiness you bring!' The strength of the handshake was so much akin to that which I had noticed in the driver, whose face I had not seen, that for a moment I doubted if it were not the same person to whom I was speaking. So to make sure, I said interrogatively, 'Count Dracula?'

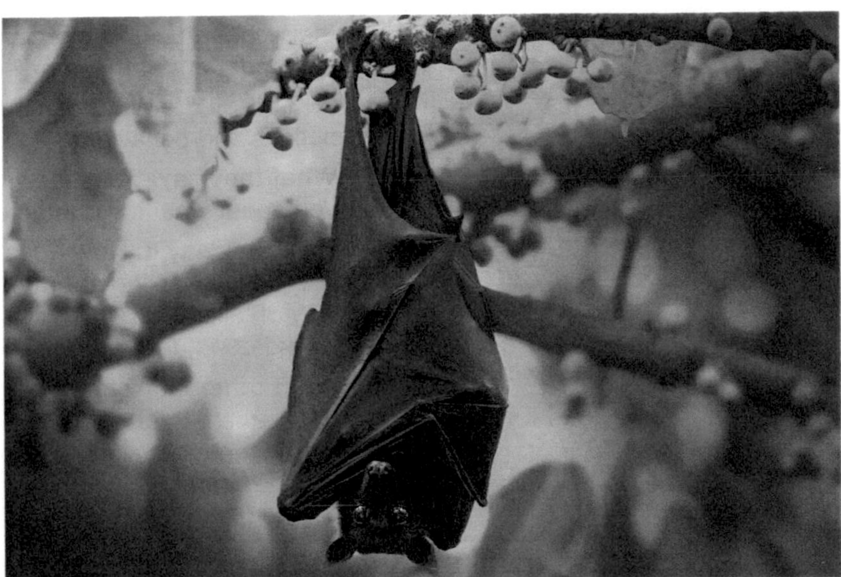

▲ Dracula is one of the most iconic figures within fiction.

ACTIVITY 2

SKILLS ANALYSIS, REASONING, INTERPRETATION

▼ BUILDING A SENSE OF CHARACTER

Read the extract from *Dracula*. How does Stoker build up a vivid sense of character in this extract? Consider his use of setting, the use of direct speech and any adjectival and adverbial descriptions. Write at least two P-E-E paragraphs about it.

ACTIVITY 3

SKILLS ANALYSIS, CREATIVITY

▼ CHARACTER DEVELOPMENT

Using the techniques you have considered, write your own short, vivid character description that begins with the description of your character's shoes. You could choose to develop your character based on the character created in Activity 1 or start with a new idea.

LEARNING OBJECTIVES

This lesson will help you to:

- select and interpret information, ideas and perspectives
- comment on the language used.

NARRATIVE VOICE

When considering a text it is important to study and discuss techniques and features of narrative, including style, plot, character, theme, viewpoint, tone and mood. A useful place to begin is to consider the 'voice' which is telling the story. Is it written in the **first person** ('I'), or **third person** (written from an external perspective separate from the characters)?

SUBJECT VOCABULARY

first person written from the perspective of one person – that is, using 'I'; this differs from the second person, which directly addresses the reader ('you'), and the third person ('he', 'she' and 'it')

third person using the third person – that is, 'he', 'she'and 'it'; this differs from the first person ('I') and the second person, which directly addresses the reader ('you')

narrator a character that tells the story in a novel, play, poem or film

ACTIVITY 1

SKILLS CRITICAL THINKING, ANALYSIS

▼ FIRST- AND THIRD- PERSON NARRATION

Whether a text is narrated in the first person or in the third person can have an impact on how a reader feels about the text. For example, a first-person narrative is more personal and a third-person narrative is more detached. Draw up a list of other differences between them.

DID YOU KNOW?

Second-person narration speaks to directly to the reader, usually referring to them as 'you'. This technique is not used very often but can make the reader feel part of the story as it invites involvement or agreement with the narrator.

CONSIDERING NARRATIVE VOICE

When thinking about narrative voice, consider these questions.

- Does the writer tell the story from a **narrator's** point of view?
- Does the writer give the reader several different points of view?
- What tone is used? For example, is it urgent, anxious, relaxed, excited?
- Do you get a sense of the narrator as a character? What details of their lives are suggested?
- Are they writing the story about themselves?
- Can you trust the narrator? Are there any clues that you should not believe everything that they say?
- Is a setting and time period established? What kinds of words are used for this?

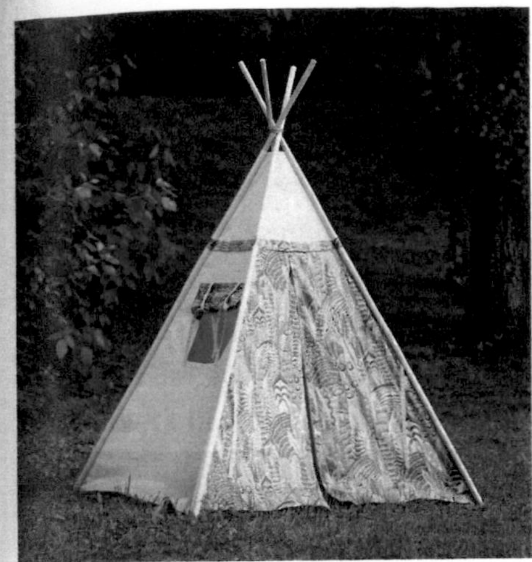

▲ A wigwam

▼ FROM *THE SALT ROAD* BY JANE JOHNSON

When I was a child, I had a wigwam in our back garden: a circle of thin yellow cotton draped over a bamboo pole and pegged to the lawn. Every time my parents argued, that was where I went. I would lie on my stomach with my fingers in my ears and stare so hard at the red animals printed on its bright decorative border that after a while they began to dance and run, until I wasn't in the garden any more but out on the plains, wearing a fringed deerskin tunic and feathers in my hair, just like the braves in the films I watched every Saturday morning in the cinema down the road.

Even at an early age I found it preferable to be outside in my little tent rather than inside the house. The tent was my space. It was as large as my imagination, which was infinite. But the house, for all its **grandeur** and **Georgian** spaciousness, felt small and suffocating. It was stuffed with things, as well as with my mother and father's bitterness. They were both **archaeologists**, my parents: lovers of the past, they had surrounded themselves with boxes of yellowed papers, ancient artefacts, dusty objects; the fragile, friable husks of lost civilizations. I never understood why they decided to have me: even the quietest baby, the most house-trained toddler, the most studious child, would have disrupted the artificial, museum-like calm they had wrapped around themselves. In that house they lived separated from the rest of the world, in a bubble in which dust motes floated silently like the fake snow in a snow-globe. I was not the child to complement such a life, being a wild little creature, loud and messy and **unbiddable**. I liked to play rough games with the boys instead of engaging in the sedate, codified exchanges of the other girls. I had dolls, but more often than not I beheaded or scalped them, or buried them in the garden and forgot where they were. I had no interest in making fashionable outfits for the **oddly attenuated** pink plastic **mannequins** with their insectile torsos and brassy hair that the other girls so worshipped and adorned.

GENERAL VOCABULARY

grandeur grandness
Georgian British style of architecture from the period 1714–1811
archaeologists scientists who study the past by looking at historical objects and sites
unbiddable will not be told what to do
oddly attenuated strangely long and thin
mannequins models or dummies

KEY POINT

The narrative voice in a text is another key part of a text. The tone can help set the mood and atmosphere and the choice of first- or third-person narration can help shape how events are reported.

ACTIVITY 2

SKILLS ▶ CRITICAL THINKING

▼ ANALYSING A NARRATIVE VOICE

Read the extract from *The Salt Road* by Jane Johnson. Highlight any information that the reader is given about the narrator in the passage. Then construct a P-E-E paragraph to answer the following question.

▶ **What sense of the narrator's home life is suggested in this passage?**

Creation of character

Read this short extract from *The Woman in White*, then answer Question 1.

"The key of the church!" I shouted to the clerk. "We must try it that way – we may save him yet if we can burst open the inner door."

"No, no, no!" cried the old man. "No hope! the church key and the vestry key are on the same ring – both inside there! Oh, sir, he's past saving – he's dust and ashes by this time!"

"They'll see the fire from the town," said a voice from among the men behind me. "There's a ingine in the town. They'll save the church."

Guided

1 In the extract above, the writer uses dialogue to create ideas about the characters. What ideas does this use of dialogue give the reader about the narrator?

The writer uses dialogue to show that the narrator is brave and impulsive ....

....

....

....

A character can be created through his or her own words, or through the words of other characters. In the extract above, 'sir' suggests that the narrator commands respect, for example.

Now read this short extract from *The Poor Relation's Story*, then answer Question 2.

As I held out my hand to him, he caught up his stick (being infirm, he always walked about the house with a stick), and made a blow at me, and said, "You fool!"
"Uncle," I returned, "I didn't expect you to be so angry as this." Nor had I expected it, though he was a hard and angry old man.
"You didn't expect!" said he; "when did you ever expect? When did you ever calculate, or look forward, you contemptible dog?"
"These are hard words, uncle!"

2 How do uncle Chill's actions and dialogue in the extract above build up an idea of both his character and the character of the narrator?

....

....

....

Turn to the full extract from *The Poor Relation's Story* on page 98. Read lines 26–31, focusing on the description of Betsy Snap. Then answer Question 3.

Character can be created through dialogue, description or action.

3 Write a P-E-E paragraph about how the writer creates ideas about the character of Betsy Snap.

....

....

....

Had a go ☐ Nearly there ☐ Nailed it! ☐

Creating atmosphere

Read this short extract from *The Poor Relation's Story,* then answer Question 1.

My life at my uncle Chill's was of a spare dull kind, and my garret chamber was as dull, and bare, and cold, as an upper prison room in some stern northern fortress. But, having Christiana's love, I wanted nothing upon earth. I would not have changed my lot with any human being.

1 The writer uses a simile to describe the narrator's room. In the answer extracts below, students have commented on the atmosphere in the text extract. They have referred to the connotations of the phrases underlined in the extract above.

A

A sad atmosphere is created by the writer using the simile of a prison room in a fortress. This suggests he is a prisoner and the room is uncomfortable and unpleasant.

B

The writer creates a sad and slightly tense atmosphere by likening the narrator's 'dull, and bare, and cold' room to a prison in a 'fortress'. This suggests that he is literally trapped like a prisoner and the use of the adjective 'stern' helps to build the tense atmosphere as it has connotations of harsh treatment.

C

The atmosphere is shown through the simile 'as an upper prison room in some stern northern fortress'. The writer also uses the adjective 'stern' to show that he is not being treated kindly.

(a) Circle the answer extract you think is the most effective (A, B or C).

(b) Explain why you feel your chosen answer extract is the most effective.

....

....

Now read this short extract, also from *The Poor Relation's Story* (lines 8–11). Then answer Questions 2 and 3.

As I came down-stairs next morning, shivering in the cold December air; colder in my uncle's unwarmed house than in the street, where the winter sun did sometimes shine, and which was at all events enlivened by cheerful faces and voices passing along; I carried a heavy heart towards the long, low breakfast-room in which my uncle sat.

2 In the extract above, the writer contrasts the inside of the house with the street outside. Identify any verbs and adjectives that create this contrast and write two or three sentences explaining how they contribute to the atmosphere created in the extract.

....

....

When you answer a question about language techniques in the exam, start with an overview to summarise the overall effect of the extract.

Guided

3 Using your answer to Question 2, write an overview sentence that sums up the overall atmosphere created in the extract above.

Overall, the writer creates an atmosphere ....

....

....

Narrative voice

Read extracts 1, 2 and 3 below.

Extract 1: from *The Woman in White*

I looked round at my two companions. The servant had risen to his feet – he had taken the lantern, and was holding it up vacantly at the door. Terror seemed to have struck him with downright idiocy – he waited at my heels, he followed me about when I moved like a dog. The clerk sat crouched up on one of the tombstones, shivering, and moaning to himself. The one moment in which I looked at them was enough to show me that they were both helpless.

Extract 2: from *The Poor Relation's Story*

As I came down-stairs next morning, shivering in the cold December air; colder in my uncle's unwarmed house than in the street, where the winter sun did sometimes shine, and which was at all events enlivened by cheerful faces and voices passing along; I carried a heavy heart towards the long, low breakfast-room in which my uncle sat.

Extract 3: from *The Return of the Native*

He was now thoroughly alarmed; and hastily putting on his clothes he descended to the front door, which he himself had bolted and locked. It was now unfastened. There was no longer any doubt that Eustacia had left the house at this midnight hour; and whither could she have gone? To follow her was almost impossible.

Now read the descriptions of narrative voice below, then answer Questions 1 and 2.

A

First person narrative has been used to give a sense of closeness to the narrator and to encourage the reader to sympathise with him.

B

Third person narrative has been used. This 'omniscient narrator' knows everything, including the narrator's thoughts and feelings.

C

First person narrative has been used to allow the reader to know the narrator's thoughts and feelings about the other characters.

Guided

1 Draw lines to link each extract (1, 2, 3) above to one of the descriptions of narrative voice (A, B, C). One has been done for you.

Narrative voice is the 'voice' a writer of fiction chooses to tell the story. A writer can choose a narrative voice to create a particular point of view.

2 Reread Extract 2. How has the first person narrative voice been used to create sympathy for the narrator?

....

....

....

....

....

....

....

Putting it into practice

Read the full extract from *The Woman in White* on page 99, then answer the exam-style question below.

Paper 

3 In lines 13–21, how does the writer use language and structure to suggest the narrator is in great danger?
Support your views with reference to the text. **(6 marks)**

When you tackle this type of question in the exam, remember to:

- spend about 12 minutes on your answer
- read the question carefully and highlight the main focus
- read the source text thoroughly, annotating as you read
- only use the lines of the text referred to in the question
- identify the language and structural devices used and comment on their effects
- support all your points with clear evidence and a clear explanation by using a P-E-E structure in your paragraphs.

In the exam you will need to write about structure to answer this kind of question. Structure is covered later in this Workbook. Here, you just need to comment on how the writer uses language – skills you have covered on pages 18–23.

. . . .

. . . .

. . . .

. . . .

. . . .

. . . .

. . . .

. . . .

. . . .

. . . .

. . . .

. . . .

. . . .

. . . .

. . . .

. . . .

. . . .

. . . .

. . . .

Remember: You have more space than this to answer your question in the exam. Use your own paper to finish your answer to the question above.

Rhetorical devices 1

Read this short extract from 'OK, you try teaching 13-year-olds', then answer Questions 1 and 2.

> Shocking news: a young trainee languages teacher on placement at Tarleton High in Lancashire "lost it" in class, barricaded the door with furniture, trapping the pupils, and threatened to kill them with something nasty that she had in her handbag. But why shocking? Imagine yourself in her place, "teaching" about 30 13- or 14-year-old creatures. Do you have one or two in your house? Are they polite, quiet and cooperative? Or are they breathtakingly insolent, noisy, crabby, offensive, skulking, smoking, drugging, and whingeing that they are not suitably entertained? What if you had 30? Wouldn't you like something in your handbag to shut the little toads up?

1 Find four of the following rhetorical devices in the extract above. Circle them below and label them in the extract.

- pattern of three
- lists
- alliteration
- rhetorical questions
- colloquial language

2 For each device you have identified, write one or two sentences commenting on:

- why the writer has used it
- the intended effect on the reader.

The answer has been started for you, with comments about the writer's use of lists.

> Remember to think about how rhetorical devices are used by considering their effect on the reader.

The writer uses a list of negative adjectives, such as 'insolent, noisy' and 'crabby' to emphasise how difficult teenagers can be. As this list comes after the description of the teacher's actions, it might make readers feel some sympathy for teachers. The writer also uses

....

....

....

....

....

....

....

....

....

....

....

....

....

Rhetorical devices 2

Read this short extract from 'We choose to go to the moon', then answer Question 1.

> Those who came before us made certain that this country rode the first waves of the industrial revolutions, the first waves of modern invention, and the first wave of nuclear power, and this generation does not intend to founder in the backwash of the coming age of space. We mean to be a part of it – we mean to lead it.

1 The writer is very persuasive about the need for space exploration. How does the repetition of the phrases 'first waves' and 'we mean' help to show this attitude?

'first waves' ....

....

'we mean' ....

....

Now read this short extract, also from 'We choose to go to the moon', lines 23–26. Then answer Question 2.

> For the eyes of the world now look into space, to the moon and to the planets beyond, and we have vowed that we shall not see it governed by a hostile flag of conquest, but by a banner of freedom and peace. We have vowed that we shall not see space filled with weapons of mass destruction, but with instruments of knowledge and understanding.

2 The underlined sections in the extract above contain contrasts (opposing or different ideas). Write one or two sentences explaining how this use of contrast helps the writer to make his point about the need for space exploration.

....

....

....

....

Read the rest of the extract from 'We choose to go to the moon' on page 102. Then answer Question 3.

> If you know it, use the technical name for the device in your answer. If you don't know the technical name, you should still comment on the language and its effect.

3 Identify one example of hyperbole and one example of emotive language in the extract. Write one or two sentences commenting on why the writer has used each rhetorical device and the effect each one has on the reader.

Hyperbole: ....

....

Emotive language: ....

....

Fact, opinion and expert evidence

Read the following three quotations from an article about teaching, then answer Question 1.

A In 2013, almost 50,000 teachers gave up teaching.

B Research from the Department for Education suggests that difficult working conditions are the main cause.

C Teaching is the most rewarding of all professions.

1 Identify which of the above extracts is:

(a) a fact ....

(b) an opinion ....

(c) expert evidence ....

Think about how the fact, opinion or expert evidence helps to support the writer's viewpoint or argument.

Now read the short extract from 'OK, you try teaching 13-year-olds' below. Then answer Questions 2 to 4.

21st

I'm trying not to sound bitter here, but I have taught; I have known supply-teaching hell; and I, too, have blown my top, even though it was 3.30pm and nearly over, because by then they were still climbing up walls (really), throwing scissors, dribbling glue and screaming all the while ... and when that happens, sometimes one just cannot keep one's cool a second longer.

And 13 is a particularly cruel age. In my first year's teaching, I crashed the car and sliced my forehead open on the sun-visor. Back at school, with my unsightly 27-stitch scar, I passed two 13-year-old girls. "She looks uglier than ever," said they, laughing merrily.

2 Write one sentence summing up the writer's viewpoint in the extract above.

....

....

3 Identify at least one fact, one opinion and one piece of expert evidence the writer uses to support her viewpoint. Highlight or underline these in the extract above.

4 Write a sentence for each example you have identified in Question 3, explaining how it supports the writer's viewpoint.

Remember that the person providing the expert evidence could be the author of the text, as in this case.

Fact: ....

....

Opinion: ....

....

Expert evidence: ....

....

Had a go ☐ Nearly there ☐ Nailed it! ☐

Identifying sentence types

Look at the sentences below, then answer Question 1.

A Teaching is not easy.

B I took some long, deep breaths until I felt ready to face the class.

C My blood ran cold and my heart stopped.

D Blind terror.

1 Look carefully at the four sentences above. Each one is a different type of sentence. But which is which?

Sentence .... is a single-clause sentence.

Sentence .... is a multi-clause sentence (coordinate).

Sentence .... is a minor sentence.

Sentence .... is a multi-clause sentence (subordinate).

Now read this short extract from 'OK, you try teaching 13-year-olds', then answer Question 2.

Now think of that young teacher. "She had been trying to get them to be quiet," we learn. So she had probably been shouted at and humiliated for 40 minutes. This was her very last day of several horrible weeks of a placement. The end of her torment was a whisker away, but, driven barmy by pupils, she still blew it. Her career is now ruined. But the children were "petrified … burst into tears" and were offered "support". The pathetic little wets. She was pretending, you fools – dredging up a last desperate ploy to shut the monsters up. If she had cried, they would have laughed out loud. Hopefully, she won't be sacked. If that's what she really, really wants.

2 In the extract above, highlight or circle one example of each kind of sentence: single-clause, multi-clause (subordinate), multi-clause (coordinate) and minor.

SINGLE-CLAUSE sentences are made up of just **one clause** and provide **one piece of information** about an event or action. They contain **a subject** and **one verb**.
MULTI-CLAUSE sentences are made up of **more than one clause**. They contain **two or more verbs**.
SUBORDINATE clauses do not make sense on their own. They are **dependent** on the main clause.
COORDINATE clauses are an **equal pair**, where neither clause is dependent on the other.
MINOR SENTENCES are grammatically incomplete because they **do not contain a verb**.

Commenting on sentence types

Read this short extract from ''Appy ever after' (lines 24–32), then answer Question 1.

He hands me the controller. I select Calm mode. I turn the dial up and – *Holy silicon mad professors!* – it hurts. There's a sharp vibration that feels like the neurons in my head are pogoing. Not relaxing at all. I turn it down and wait. And then something remarkable happens. After a few minutes, I begin to feel waves gently flowing through my head. I don't notice at first but soon I begin to slump in my chair, my pupils dilate and my breathing slows.

1 The extract above starts with short, single-clause sentences and ends with a long, multi-clause sentence that has several subordinate clauses. How do these sentence structures suggest what is happening to the narrator's feelings?

....

....

....

Now read this short extract from *The Return of the Native*, in which Clym realises that Eustacia has gone. Then answer Question 2.

19th

He went on to the landing, and stood waiting nearly five minutes. Still she did not return. He went back for a light, and prepared to follow her; but first he looked into her bedroom. There, on the outside of the quilt, was the impression of her form, showing that the bed had not been opened; and, what was more significant, she had not taken her candlestick downstairs. He was now thoroughly alarmed; and hastily putting on his clothes he descended to the front door, which he himself had bolted and locked. It was now unfastened.

Guided

2 In this extract, the writer uses a variety of sentence lengths to create a sense of suspense about Eustacia's disappearance. Explain how the sentence structures create suspense.

The writer starts the paragraph by explaining where and for how long the narrator waited. This is immediately followed by a short, single-clause sentence starting with the word 'still', which creates suspense because ....

....

....

After this short, single-clause sentence, the writer then uses several longer, multi-clause sentences followed by another short, single-clause sentence. This adds to the suspense ...

....

....

Turn to the full extract from *The Return of the Native* on page 96, and read lines 6–12. Then answer Question 3.

3 Write one or two sentences explaining how the sentence structure continues to build suspense.

....

....

....

....

Had a go ☐ Nearly there ☐ Nailed it! ☐

Structure: non-fiction

Read this short extract from 'OK, you try teaching 13-year-olds' by Michele Hanson, then answer Question 1.

> Shocking news: a young trainee languages teacher on placement at Tarleton High in Lancashire "lost it" in class, barricaded the door with furniture, trapping the pupils, and threatened to kill them with something nasty that she had in her handbag.

1 The opening of any text needs to engage the reader. In the extract above, the writer chooses to use the opening to set the scene. How has she ensured that readers will want to read on?

....

....

Now read the full extract from 'OK, you try teaching 13-year-olds' on page 101. Then answer Question 2.

2 Consider the following ways in which writers can end their writing in order to leave a lasting impression:

vivid images	warnings	calls to action	positivity	summary of main points made

Circle the one you think most suits the way Michele Hanson ends her article and explain why you think she chose to end it that way.

....

....

Read this short extract from the article ''Appy ever after' by John Arlidge:

21st

> The trouble is, Goldwasser has just attached two electrodes to my head and is about to start pumping electricity straight into my brain.

Now read this second short extract, from later in the same article, before answering Question 3. The electricity is now flowing through the electrodes into Arlidge's head:

> And then something remarkable happens. After a few minutes I begin to feel waves gently flowing through my head. I don't notice at first but soon I begin to slump in my chair, my pupils dilate and my breathing slows.

Guided

3 Writers need to keep the interest of their readers and they often do it by changing the tone in the middle section of their writing. How does Arlidge do this in the extracts from his article above?

Initially, Arlidge is scared about the idea of having two electrodes attached to his head. This is implied in the phrase 'pumping electricity straight into my brain'. However, when he actually tries the electrodes, his tone changes ....

....

....

....

....

Structure: fiction

Read the full extract from *The Poor Relation's Story* on page 98. Now focus on these lines from the extract and then answer Question 1.

Avarice was, unhappily, my uncle Chill's master-vice. Though he was rich, he pinched, and scraped, and clutched, and lived miserably. As Christiana had no fortune, I was for some time a little fearful of confessing our engagement to him; but, at length I wrote him a letter, saying how it all truly was. I put it into his hand one night, on going to bed.

Guided

1 How does the sentence underlined in the short extract above foreshadow uncle Chill's reaction, later in the full extract, to the engagement?

The words 'fearful' and 'confessing' in the lines above suggest that the narrator knows his uncle will ....

....

....

Now read this short extract (lines 13–16) from *The Return of the Native*, then answer Question 2.

At half-past eleven, finding that the house was silent, Eustacia had lighted her candle, put on some warm outer wrappings, taken her bag in her hand, and, extinguishing the light again, descended the staircase. When she got into the outer air she found that it had begun to rain, and as she stood pausing at the door it increased, threatening to come on heavily.

2 Here, the writer describes Eustacia's actions in detail. What is the effect of this structure on the reader?

....

....

....

....

....

Read the full extract from *The Return of the Native* on page 96, focusing on the final paragraph (lines 31–39). Now reread the short extract on this page that you explored in Question 2. Then answer Question 3.

3 How does the close description of the action in the short extract above serve as a build-up to Eustacia's realisation about money in the final paragraph?

....

....

....

....

Remember that writers of fiction use a variety of narrative structures for effect. These include foreshadowing, use of closely described detail or action, repetition and dialogue.

Had a go ☐ Nearly there ☐ Nailed it! ☐

Putting it into practice

Read the full extract from *The Woman in White* on page 99, then answer the exam-style question below.

Paper 1

3 In lines 31–38, how does the writer use language and structure to suggest the narrator's determination to save the trapped man?
Support your views with reference to the text. **(6 marks)**

When you tackle this type of question in the exam, remember to:

- spend around 12 minutes on your answer
- read the question carefully and highlight the main focus
- read the source text thoroughly, annotating as you read
- only use the lines of the text referred to in the question
- identify the language and structural devices used and comment on their effects
- support all your points with clear evidence and a clear explanation by using a P-E-E structure in your paragraphs.

Note that in the exam you will also need to write about language to answer this kind of question. You practised this on page 24 of this Workbook. Here, however, just practise commenting on how the writer uses sentences and structure – skills you have covered on pages 28, 29 and 31.

Remember: You have more space than this to answer your question in the exam. Use your own paper to finish your answer to the question above.

Putting it into practice

Read the full extract from 'Dear daughter' on page 100, then answer the exam-style question below.

Paper 

3 Analyse how the writer uses language and structure to interest and engage readers. Support your views with detailed reference to the text. **(15 marks)**

When you tackle this type of question in the exam, remember to:

- spend about 15 minutes on your answer
- read the text carefully and annotate it with your ideas
- refer to the whole text as no line numbers are given
- identify the language and structural techniques used and comment on their effects
- support all your points with clear evidence and a clear explanation by using a P-E-E structure in your paragraphs.

Remember: You have more space than this to answer your question in the exam. Use your own paper to finish your answer to the question above.

Had a go ☐ Nearly there ☐ Nailed it! ☐

Handling two texts

In Paper 2, two assessment objectives will test your ability to handle two texts together. These are Assessment objectives 1 (b) and 3. Read the assessment objectives, then answer Questions 1 and 2.

Assessment objective 1 (b)

Select and synthesise evidence from different texts

Assessment objective 3

Compare writers' ideas and perspectives, as well as how these are conveyed, across two or more texts

1 Circle the word below which is **not** a synonym for 'synthesise'.

combine | fuse | amalgamate | blend | mix | separate

The texts in Paper 2 may be similar or different in various ways. Think about:
- the ideas they express about the topic
- the language they use
- their points of view
- how they are structured.

2 Which of the assessment objectives above will require you to identify **and** explain both similarities **and** differences between the two texts? ....

Now look at these exam-style questions. **You don't need to answer these questions**. Instead, think about how they test the skills in Assessment objectives 1 (b) and 3 and then answer Question 3.

Paper

7 **(a)** The two texts are both about school life.
What are the similarities between life in the two schools?
Use evidence from both texts to support your answer. **(6 marks)**

(b) Compare how the writers of 'OK, you try teaching 13-year-olds' and *Bad Blood* present their ideas and perspectives about teachers.
Support your answer with detailed reference to the texts. **(14 marks)**

3 Read the statements below. Decide which paper or question each statement describes. Circle your choices.

(a) The two non-fiction texts will always be linked by a common theme or topic, so they will always have something in common. **Paper 1 Paper 2**

(b) This question will test Assessment objective 3 by asking you to compare the texts. **Question 7 (a) Question 7 (b)**

(c) This question will test Assessment objective 1 (b) by asking you to synthesise information from both texts. **Question 7 (a) Question 7 (b)**

(d) This question is worth only 6 marks, so you should only make about three or four points. **Question 7 (a) Question 7 (b)**

(e) This question is worth 14 marks, so you should spend more time on this question. **Question 7 (a) Question 7 (b)**

(f) For this question, you will need to compare the language used as well as looking at the writers' attitudes and ideas. **Question 7 (a) Question 7 (b)**

(g) For this question, you should start by giving an overview to show your understanding of the question. **Question 7 (a) Question 7 (b)**

Selecting evidence for synthesis

Read the full extracts from 'OK, you try teaching 13-year-olds' by Michele Hanson on page 101 and *Bad Blood* by Lorna Sage on page 105. Then read the exam-style question below. **You don't need to answer this question**. Instead, think about what it is asking you to do, then answer Question 1.

Paper 2

7 (a) The two texts are about the relationship between students and their teacher.
What similarities are there between the relationships described by Hanson and Sage?
Use evidence from both texts to support your answer. **(6 marks)**

Only 6 marks are available for this question, so skim read the texts to save time.

Guided

1 Both texts suggest that relationships between teachers and students are difficult. Write out one piece of evidence from each text that supports this similarity. The first one has been done for you.

'OK, you try teaching 13-year-olds': 'a young trainee languages teacher ... "lost it" in class, barricaded the door with furniture, trapping the pupils, and threatened to kill them with something nasty that she had in her handbag'.

Bad Blood: ....

....

When you have found evidence in the first text, select evidence from the second text that you can combine with it.

Read the exam-style question below. **You don't need to answer this question**. Instead, think about what it is asking you to do, then answer Questions 2 and 3.
Question relating to the text extracts 'Dear daughter' and *Unreliable Memoirs*.

Paper 2

7 (a) The two texts are about the risks taken by young people.
What similarities are there between the risky behaviours of the young people?
Use evidence from both texts to support your answer. **(6 marks)**

2 Underline or highlight the key words in Question 7 (a) above.

3 Look at the short extracts below. Which ones would be a good source of relevant quotations in answer to Question 7 (a) above? Circle one extract from each text.

(a) Extracts from 'Dear daughter'

i Please think before you press 'send' on a provocative image. Think about who will see it and what it says about you.

ii In my day of course, before we all had smartphones and still communicated via pigeons and slates, it wasn't an issue.

(b) Extracts from *Unreliable memoirs*

i Organised a spectacular finish in which the riders had to plunge into my mother's prize privet hedge.

ii Not for the only time, I heard her tell me that I was more than she could cope with.

Had a go ☐ Nearly there ☐ Nailed it! ☐

Synthesising evidence

When you are synthesising the evidence you have selected from the two non-fiction texts in Paper 2, you need to use suitable adverbials and linking phrases.

Guided

1 Tick or circle the adverbials and linking phrases below that are suitable for synthesising evidence. Two examples have been done for you.

similarly	on the other hand	(likewise)	both writers feel	in the same way	however	(both texts suggest)

2 Why should you use adverbials and linking phrases in your synthesis of evidence?

....

....

To show your full understanding of the synthesis question, you should start your answer with an overview. Read the exam-style question below. **You don't need to answer this question now**. Instead, think about what it is asking you to do, then answer Question 3.

Paper 2

7 (a) The two texts are about the risks taken by young people.
What similarities are there between the risky behaviours of the young people?
Use evidence from both texts to support your answer. **(6 marks)**

3 Look at the overviews below, which students have written in response to Question 7 (a) above.

A Both writers write about young people.

B Both writers write about young people: one is written by a mother and one is from the viewpoint of a child.

C Both texts suggest that young people take risks that cause their parents to worry.

(a) Tick or circle the overview that you think is most effective.

(b) Explain why the overview you have chosen would be the best way to start an answer to Question 7 (a) above.

....

....

4 Read the full extracts from 'Dear daughter' by Jo Middleton on page 100 and *Unreliable Memoirs* by Clive James on page 104. Then write one synthesis paragraph in answer to Question 7 (a) above.

- Use suitable adverbials and linking phrases from the selection at the top of this page.
- Start your paragraph with the overview you chose for Question 3.
- You could use the evidence you identified on page 35.

....

....

....

....

....

....

Try to make each sentence cover both texts. Use short quotations where possible, or paraphrase the text if a quotation would be too long.

Looking closely at language

Read this short extract from ''Appy ever after', then answer Questions 1 to 3.

> Goldwasser and Tyler may sound bonkers, but if their timing is anything to go by, they're the smartest guys in the lab. Wearable gizmos are the hottest new sector in the trillion-pound global technology sector. Apple launches its first smartwatch in the new year and will be followed by wearable kit from Microsoft and Google, which promises new versions of its web-enabled spectacles, Google Glass. Many of the new devices are designed to improve our health by monitoring our blood pressure and our stress levels, keeping tabs on how much exercise we take and helping us to feel refreshed in the morning by waking us up as we are coming out of a period of deep sleep.

Guided

1 What are the connotations of the words and phrases circled in the extract above? The first one has been done for you.

'bonkers' means 'mad', 'crazy' or 'wild'. It's an informal term so it could have positive connotations.

'gizmos' ....

'wearable kit' ....

2 Write one or two sentences explaining the effect created by the words and phrases circled in the extract. Use the words and phrases as quotations and make sure you refer to their connotations.

....

....

....

3 The final sentence (underlined in the extract above) is very long and has several subordinate clauses. How does this sentence change the tone of this short extract?

....

....

....

Now read this short extract, also from ''Appy ever after', then answer Question 4.

21st

> Goldwasser and Tyler are taking the idea one step further, giving us the power to change the way we feel, whenever we want.
>
> "Tap into your self-control. Tap into your creativity. Tap into your energy. Tap into your calm. Think of us as your third cup of coffee in the morning or your glass of wine at night," Goldwasser smiles.

4 Look at the language and sentence structure in the extract above.

(a) Identify the rhetorical device used. Write a sentence commenting on the effect it creates.

....

....

(b) Explain the effect created by the sentence structure.

....

....

When answering a comparison question you must not write about one text without making a comparison point about the other. You should always look for similarities and differences between the two texts and try to give the texts equal weighting in your answer.

Had a go ☐ Nearly there ☐ Nailed it! ☐

Planning to compare

Read the short extracts 1 and 2 below. Then answer Question 1.

Extract 1: from *Bad Blood*

I did all right with something beginning with B (Bolton or Blackburn or Birkenhead or Birmingham) but I cried anyway, I always did. Although we may not have found out much about geography that day, we were being taught a lesson, the usual one: to know our place. Hanmer wasn't on the map and Hanmer was where we were. Most of us, according to Mr Palmer, would be muck shovellers. Two or three of us, equally pawns in the game, would be allowed to get away with it – this time.

Extract 2: from 'OK, you try teaching 13-year-olds'

I'm trying not to sound bitter here, but I have taught; I have known supply-teaching hell; and I, too, have blown my top, even though it was 3.30pm and nearly over, because by then they were still climbing up walls (really), throwing scissors, dribbling glue and screaming all the while … and when that happens, sometimes one just cannot keep one's cool a second longer.

And 13 is a particularly cruel age. In my first year's teaching, I crashed the car and sliced my forehead open on the sun-visor. Back at school, with my unsightly 27-stitch scar, I passed two 13-year-old girls. "She looks uglier than ever," said they, laughing merrily.

Guided **1** Now look at one student's plan for comparing the language in the two texts, and its effects. The plan is incomplete. Add as many details as you can, for example, quotations and explanations.

When comparing you can:

- start with the language and structural techniques the texts have in common, then compare the effects created

OR

- start with similarities in the effects of the two texts (for example, tone), then compare the techniques the writers have used to create these effects.

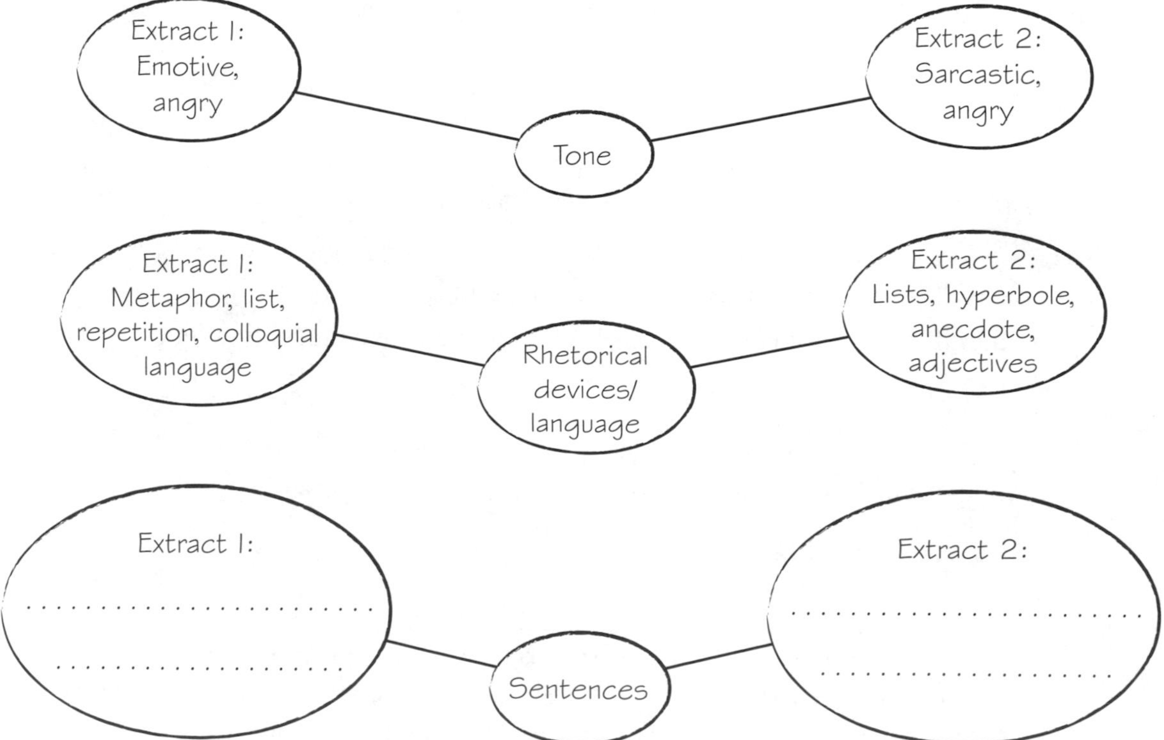

Comparing ideas and perspectives

Read the openings to 'Dear daughter' by Suzanne Whitton, lines 5–7, full text on page 100, and *Unreliable Memoirs* by Clive James, lines 1–6, full text on page 104. Then answer Question 1.

Guided

1 Finish this sentence, identifying and comparing the main ideas in the two openings.

Both texts start by expressing ideas about ....

....

Now read these short extracts below. Then answer Question 2.

Extract 1: from 'Dear daughter'

21st

You might think this barmy old dinosaur doesn't get it. I do. So please give my words a chance.

Extract 2: from *Unreliable Memoirs*

20th

She chased me up the peach tree and hit me around the ankles with a willow wand. It didn't hurt me as much as her tears did. Not for the only time, I heard her tell me that I was more than she could cope with.

2 Extract 1 suggests that the writer is sympathetic to the risks taken by young people. How does James's perspective compare with this? Use evidence from Extract 2 in your answer.

....

....

....

Now read the full extracts from 'Dear daughter' on page 100 and *Unreliable Memoirs* on page 104. Pay particular attention to the way they end. Then answer Question 3.

It is a good idea to look at differences between the beginning and end of a text when you are thinking about ideas and perspectives. This will also help you to compare the structure of the texts.

3 Write a paragraph comparing the writers' perspectives throughout the extracts. Use your answers to Questions 1 and 2 above and consider whether the writers' perspectives remain the same throughout. Use one piece of evidence from each of the extracts in your answer.

....

....

....

....

....

....

....

Had a go ☐ Nearly there ☐ Nailed it! ☐

Answering a comparison question

When you compare the language used in two texts you can write about:

The main idea: what the texts are about

Both texts are about ...

On the other hand, **Extract 2** explores ...

Extract 1 is about ...

The perspective: the writers' point of view

The writer of **Extract 1** feels ...

The language in **Extract 1** suggests that the writer feels ...

The perspective of the writer is ...

The perspective is shown through the writer's use of ...

negative

positive

The effect on the reader:

Both texts aim to engage the reader but do so in different ways.

Extract 1 engages the reader by ...

Extract 2, however, uses ...

create humour

influence

shock

Similar language features:

Both texts use rhetorical questions, but use them to achieve different effects.

Extract 1 poses the question ...

Extract 2 uses a rhetorical question to ...

lists

pattern of three

figurative language

contrast

repetition

emotive language

hyperbole

sentence

structure

Remember to make direct comparisons and make sure that you can compare similarities and differences between the two texts.

1 Reread the full extracts from 'OK, you try teaching 13-year-olds' on page 101 and *Bad Blood* on page 105. Use the prompts above to write a paragraph comparing the different ways language and structure are used for effect in the two extracts. Use the details you added to the plan on page 38 and remember to use quotations as evidence to support your points.

....

....

....

....

....

....

Putting it into practice

Read the full extracts from 'Dear daughter' on page 100 and *Unreliable Memoirs* on page 104, then answer the exam-style question below.

Paper 2

7 (b) Compare how the writers of 'Dear daughter' and *Unreliable Memoirs* present their ideas and perspectives about the relationship between children and their mothers. Support your answer with detailed reference to the texts. **(14 marks)**

When you tackle this type of question in the exam, remember to:

- spend about 14 minutes on your answer
- read the question carefully and highlight the main focus
- spend a couple of minutes planning your answer before you start writing
- refer to the whole of each text to find points relevant to the question
- always write about both texts throughout your answer
- identify the language and structural techniques used and comment on how they help the writer to get across their ideas and arguments.

Remember: You have more space than this to answer your question in the exam. Use your own paper to finish your answer to the question above.

Had a go ☐ Nearly there ☐ Nailed it! ☐

Evaluating a text

Both papers will require you to evaluate a text.

1 Circle the word below which is **not** a synonym for 'evaluate'.

form an opinion of | analyse | assess | judge | weigh up | summarise

Guided

2 Read the following statements about evaluation and decide whether they are true or false. Circle your choices. One has been done for you.

(a) You need to look closely at the connotations of individual words/phrases.	TRUE	FALSE
(b) You need to look at the text as a whole.	TRUE	FALSE
(c) It is a good idea to look at ideas, themes, events and settings.	TRUE	FALSE
(d) You should always write about ideas, themes, events and settings for every text you are asked to evaluate.	TRUE	(FALSE)
(e) You must use exact quotations from the text as evidence.	TRUE	FALSE
(f) The questions will have a specific focus.	TRUE	FALSE

3 Write a sentence explaining why part (d) above is false.

....

....

Paper 1

4 When you approach an evaluation question you should identify any **ideas, events, themes** and **settings** that are relevant to the question.

(a) Draw lines to match the evaluative areas to their descriptions.

A Ideas	**i** Where and when things happen.
B Events	**ii** Think about the text's tone or purpose.
C Themes	**iii**
D Settings	**iv** What happens or is described.

Consider all four evaluative areas when you read an extract, but only write about them if they are relevant. For example, settings may not be relevant for a non-fiction text.

(b) Write the description that is missing in question part (a) above.

5 Complete the table below, describing your approach to the two exam-style questions. **You do not need to answer the exam-style questions**.

Paper 1	Paper 2
4 In this extract, there is an attempt to present the narrator as brave. Evaluate how successfully this is achieved. Support your views with detailed reference to the text. **(15 marks)**	**6** Clive James attempts to entertain the reader with descriptions of his youthful exploits. Evaluate how successfully this is achieved. Support your views with detailed reference to the text. **(15 marks)**
How long to spend on answer:	**How long to spend on answer:**
Focus of question:	**Focus of question:**
I'll need to look at (tick the best option): • an effect that is created in the extract • one specific aspect of the extract.	**I'll need to look at (tick the best option):** • an effect that is created in the extract • one specific aspect of the extract.

Evaluating a text: fiction

Read this short extract from the opening of *The Poor Relation's Story*. Look at how the description of the setting is used for effect and to build sympathy for the narrator.

> My life at my uncle Chill's was of a spare dull kind, and my garret chamber was as dull, and bare, and cold, as an upper prison room in some stern northern fortress. But, having Christiana's love, I wanted nothing upon earth. I would not have changed my lot with any human being. ...
> As I came down-stairs next morning, shivering in the cold December air; colder in my uncle's unwarmed house than in the street, where the winter sun did sometimes shine, and which was at all events enlivened by cheerful faces and voices passing along; I carried a heavy heart towards the long, low breakfast-room in which my uncle sat.

Now read the exam-style question below. **You don't need to answer this question**. Instead, think about what it is asking you to do, then answer Questions 1 to 3.

> 4 In this extract, there is an attempt to build sympathy for the narrator.
> Evaluate how successfully this is achieved.
> Support your views with detailed reference to the text. **(15 marks)**

Guided **1** Underline references to the setting in the short extract above that would be useful when answering exam-style Question 4. An example has been done for you.

Guided **2** Complete the following P-E-E paragraph about the setting in the short extract above. Add appropriate evidence, using your answer to Question 1, and explain how this builds sympathy for the narrator.

The setting builds sympathy for the narrator as it is presented by the writer as harsh.

....

....

....

....

Now read the full extract from *The Poor Relation's Story* on page 98. Consider how **events** are used for effect. What happens to make the reader feel sympathy for the narrator?

3 Note down at least three events that create sympathy for the narrator.

....

....

....

4 Now use the events you have listed for Question 3 to write a P-E-E paragraph evaluating how these events build sympathy for the narrator.

....

....

....

....

....

> Settings and events are usually most relevant in a fiction text, but you could look at the ideas and themes, too. Remember – you don't need to analyse language or structure in detail when evaluating.

Had a go ☐ Nearly there ☐ Nailed it! ☐

Evaluating a text: non-fiction

Read this short extract from the opening of *Unreliable Memoirs*. Look at how the ideas and themes are used to entertain the reader.

Such catastrophes distressed my mother but she wrote them off as growing pains. Other exploits broke her heart. Once when she was out shopping I was riding my second-hand bike Malvern Star 26-inch frame bicycle around the house on a complicated circuit which led from the back yard along the driveway, once around a small fir tree that stood in the front yard, and back along the narrow side passage. Passing boys noticed what I was up to and came riding in. In a while there were a dozen or so of us circulating endlessly against the clock.

Idea: risky behaviour

Now read the exam-style question below. **You don't need to answer this question**. Instead, think about what it is asking you to do, then answer Question 1.

Paper

6 Clive James attempts to entertain the reader with descriptions of his youthful exploits. Evaluate how successfully this is achieved.
Support your views with detailed reference to the text. **(15 marks)**

Guided 1 What are the main ideas in this opening that would be useful when answering exam-style Question 6? Annotate the extract, underlining the evidence and naming the ideas. An example has been done for you.

Now read this short extract, also from *Unreliable Memoirs.* Think about the themes in the extract, then answer Question 2.

Themes are similar to ideas. You could think of themes as the tone or purpose of the text. Ideas and themes are likely to be most relevant in a non-fiction text. However, for some non-fiction texts it may also be useful to look at events and settings.

I organised a spectacular finish in which the riders had to plunge into my mother's prize privet hedge. The idea was for the bike's front wheel to lodge in the thick privet and the rider to fall dramatically into the bush and disappear. It became harder and harder to disappear as the privet became more and more reduced to ruins.

2 One theme in the extract from *Unreliable Memoirs* is humour, as Clive James is attempting to entertain the reader. Underline evidence of humour in the short extract above.

Now read the full extract from *Unreliable Memoirs* on page 104, then answer Questions 3 and 4.

3 As it is a memoir, *Unreliable Memoirs* covers a series of specific events. Make a list of the events in the extract.

. . . .

. . . .

. . . .

4 Write a P-E-E paragraph evaluating how successful James is in his attempt to entertain the reader. You could use some of your answers to Questions 1, 2 and 3 in your paragraph.

. . . .

. . . .

. . . .

Putting it into practice

Read the full extract from *The Return of the Native* on page 96, then answer the exam-style question below.

Paper 1

4 In this extract, there is an attempt to build suspense.
Evaluate how successfully this is achieved.
Support your views with detailed reference to the text. **(15 marks)**

When you tackle this type of question in the exam, remember to:

- spend around 30 minutes on your answer
- read the question carefully and highlight the main focus
- refer to the whole text, reading it thoroughly and annotating as you read
- look at how ideas, events, themes and settings are used to create effects
- use inference and evidence from the text to explain your ideas and assess the effect of the text.

Remember: You have more space than this to answer your question in the exam. Use your own paper to finish your answer to the question above.

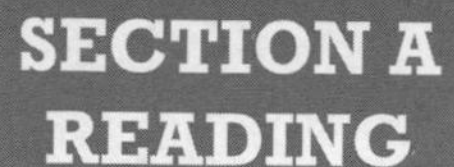

Had a go ☐ Nearly there ☐ Nailed it! ☐

Putting it into practice

Read the full extract from 'We choose to go to the moon' on page 102, then answer the exam-style question below.

Paper 2

6 Kennedy attempts to engage his audience through his descriptions of man's achievements and his hopes for future achievements.
Evaluate how successfully this is achieved.
Support your views with detailed reference to the text. **(15 marks)**

When you tackle this type of question in the exam, remember to:

- spend around 15 minutes on your answer
- read the question carefully and highlight the main focus
- refer to the whole text, reading it thoroughly and annotating as you read
- look at how ideas, events, themes and settings are used to create effects
- use inference and evidence from the text to explain your ideas and assess the effect of the text.

Remember: You have more space than this to answer your question in the exam. Use your own paper to finish your answer to the question above.

Writing questions: an overview

Both papers of the English Language GCSE include a writing section: Section B.

1 Read the statements below. Decide which paper – or papers – each statement describes. Circle your choices.

(a) The writing focus is imaginative writing.	**Paper 1**	**Paper 2**	**Both**
(b) The writing focus is transactional writing.	**Paper 1**	**Paper 2**	**Both**
(c) The writing section tests your ability to write for different purposes and audiences.	**Paper 1**	**Paper 2**	**Both**
(d) You will be given a choice of two tasks.	**Paper 1**	**Paper 2**	**Both**
(e) The writing tasks will be linked by a theme to the reading extracts in Section A.	**Paper 1**	**Paper 2**	**Both**

Assessment objective 5

(a) Communicate clearly, effectively and imaginatively, selecting and adapting tone, style and register for different forms, purposes and audiences

(b) Organise information and ideas, using structural and grammatical features to support coherence and cohesion of texts

Assessment objective 6

Use a range of vocabulary and sentence structures for clarity, purpose and effect, with accurate spelling and punctuation

2 Now read these statements about the assessment objectives tested in the writing sections. Decide which of the assessment objectives above each statement belongs to. Circle your choices.

(a) Tests how well you can use sentences and paragraphs to structure and organise your writing effectively.	**AO5**	**AO6**	**Both**
(b) Tests your vocabulary and whether you can use sentence structures for effect.	**AO5**	**AO6**	**Both**
(c) Tests your spelling and punctuation.	**AO5**	**AO6**	**Both**
(d) Tests your ability to write in different forms, and for different purposes and audiences.	**AO5**	**AO6**	**Both**

Guided

3 Summarise each assessment objective into one short sentence without using the words that are circled in the descriptions above.

Assessment objective 5 (a) ....

....

Assessment objective 5 (b) Arrange ....

....

Assessment objective 6 ....

....

Putting things into your own words and summarising ideas is a good revision technique. If you can summarise effectively, it shows that you fully understand what you are reading.

Had a go ☐ Nearly there ☐ Nailed it! ☐

Writing questions: Paper 1

Paper 1 tests your imaginative writing skills.

1 Read the statements about Paper 1 below. Decide whether each statement is true or false. Circle your choices.

(a) The questions will tell you which form your writing should take. **True False**

(b) You should write in prose. **True False**

(c) There will be two types of question to choose from. **True False**

(d) It is a good idea to plan your answer before you start to write. **True False**

Look at the exam-style questions below. **You don't need to answer these questions**. Instead, think about what they are asking you to do, then answer Questions 2 and 3.

Paper 1

5 Write about a time when you, or someone you know, lost something valuable.
Your response could be real or imagined. **(40 marks)**

6 Look at images A and B on page 106.
Write about being watched.
Your response could be real or imagined. You may wish to base your response on one of the images. **(40 marks)**

There is a total of 40 marks available for the writing section of Paper 1:

- a maximum of 24 marks are awarded for Assessment objective 5 (communication and organisation)
- a maximum of 16 marks are awarded for Assessment objective 6 (spelling, punctuation, grammar and vocabulary).

Turn to page 47 for a reminder about the assessment objectives.

2 Your imaginative writing does not need to be based on something that has actually happened. Circle the phrase that makes this clear in both exam-style questions.

3 Which word in exam-style Question 6 tells you that you do not have to base your writing on one of the images?

....

The table below shows three vital stages of answering a Paper 1 writing task.

Guided

4 Complete the table by writing the number of minutes you could spend on each stage. The first row has been done for you.

Total time for Paper 1: Section B – Writing	45 minutes
Planning your answer	
Writing your answer	
Checking and proofreading your answer	

Writing questions: Paper 2

Paper 2 tests your skills in transactional writing.

Guided

1 Cross out the incorrect words or phrases from the pairs below. Two examples have been done for you.

Transactional writing is usually:

- formal / ~~informal~~
- intended to achieve a specific purpose / amusing and light-hearted
- entertaining and humorous / serious, with humour only if appropriate to audience
- for a specific audience / suitable for all ages
- ~~open-ended~~ / carefully structured

Paper 2 questions are worth 40 marks:

- a maximum of 24 marks are awarded for Assessment objective 5 (communication and organisation)
- a maximum of 16 marks are awarded for Assessment objective 6 (spelling, punctuation, grammar and vocabulary).

Turn to page 47 for a reminder about the assessment objectives.

Look at the exam-style questions below. **You don't need to answer these questions.** Instead, consider what they are asking you to do, then answer Question 2.

Paper 2

8 Write a report for your Headteacher/Principal suggesting ways in which the school could encourage healthy eating.

In your report, you could:

- state why healthy eating is important for both students and staff
- describe what type of food is eaten at the moment and what problems this causes
- suggest how the school could encourage students and staff to become healthy eaters

as well as any other ideas you may have. **(40 marks)**

Paper 2

9 Write an article for your local newspaper, exploring the idea that local fast food restaurants should stop serving customers under the age of 18.

You could write about:

- the types of fast food restaurants in the area and the types of food they offer
- why customers under the age of 18 might want to use the restaurants
- the advantages and disadvantages of preventing young people from using the restaurants

as well as any other ideas you may have. **(40 marks)**

2 (a) Circle the words in Question 8 that tell you which audience you should be writing for.

(b) Circle the words in each question that tell you the form your writing should take.

(c) Circle the words in each question that tell you, or suggest to you, what the purpose of your writing should be.

3 You have a total of 45 minutes for the Writing section in Paper 2. Complete the table by writing in the timings for each stage of your answer.

	Start writing at 11.00 am
Planning your answer	11.00 –
Writing your answer	
Checking and proofreading your answer	

Always leave enough time to check your answer thoroughly.

Had a go ☐ Nearly there ☐ Nailed it! ☐

Writing for a purpose: imaginative

Look at the exam-style question below. **You don't need to answer this question now**. Instead, think about what you might include in a response to this title, then answer Questions 1 to 4.

Paper 1

5 Write about a time when you, or someone you know, had an exciting day out at a theme park.
Your response could be real or imagined. **(40 marks)**

Guided

1 Using the senses can help you to create a vivid picture in a reader's mind. Complete the table below to gather ideas you could use in your answer to the exam-style question above. An idea has been added for you.

Walking towards the theme park, the first thing I noticed was ...

see:	
hear:	
smell:	the sharp tang of diesel oil on the breeze
touch:	
taste:	

When you describe feelings, try to use verbs that show, rather than tell, the reader. This will make your writing more engaging.

Guided

2 The exam-style question above could be answered in the first person. This would allow you to describe feelings in detail. Finish this sentence about how you were feeling at the theme park:

My face lit up with a wide smile and ....
....
....

Remember to keep the same narrative voice throughout your answer in the exam.

3 Figurative language will also help you to create strong descriptions and vivid images. Use these figurative devices to describe three things at the theme park (e.g. a ride, the noise, the queues).

Simile: ....

Metaphor: ....

Personification: ....

Using fewer well-chosen words is more effective than using too many unimaginative ones.

4 Write the first three sentences of your answer to the exam-style question at the top of this page. Use your answers to Questions 1 to 3 in your writing. Remember to choose your vocabulary carefully and try to use verbs that show rather than tell your feelings.

....
....
....
....
....
....
....

Writing for a purpose: inform, explain, review

Look at the exam-style question below. **You don't need to answer this question now**. Instead, think about what you might include in a response to this title, then answer Questions 1 to 3.

8 Write a report for your local council, suggesting ways in which they could encourage more young people to use the library.

In your report you could:

- suggest reasons why young people might not be using the library, e.g. what they are doing instead, what is wrong with the library
- give examples of what could be improved at the library to encourage young people to use it
- describe your ideas about how the council could publicise the library and its facilities to young people

as well as any other ideas you might have. **(40 marks)**

Texts that inform, explain or review are all examples of transactional writing.

Guided

1 Transactional writing often uses headings and subheadings to guide the reader and make the information easier to find. List up to four subheadings that you could use to organise your answer to exam-style Question 8. An example has been done for you.

(a) ....

(b) ....

(c) Using social media to attract teenagers to the library

(d) ....

2 Using facts and statistics is an effective way to make your writing appear reliable. Write down four facts or statistics that you could include in your answer to exam-style Question 8.

(a) ....

(b) ....

(c) ....

(d) ....

Remember that the questions in Paper 2: Section B – Writing will be linked by theme to the reading texts in Section A. This means that you may be able to use facts and statistics from one or both of these texts. You can make up facts and statistics too, as long as they are believable and appropriate.

3 Using the correct tone in your transactional writing is very important. Texts that inform, explain or review usually have a formal tone as they need to sound trustworthy. Write the opening paragraph of your answer to exam-style Question 8. Use a formal tone and try to use one of your headings from Question 1 and some of the facts and statistics from your answer to Question 2.

....

....

....

....

In transactional writing, avoid using too much figurative language.

Writing for a purpose: argue and persuade

Look at the exam-style question below. **You don't need to answer this question**. Instead, think about what you might include in a response to this title, then answer Questions 1 to 4.

Paper

9 Write an article for a national newspaper, exploring the idea that the internet is addictive and harmful.

You could write about:

- the way people use the internet, e.g. business, social, online shopping
- the advantages and disadvantages of the internet
- how the internet can be used safely and/or whether its use should be limited

as well as any other ideas you might have. **(40 marks)**

1 Decide whether or not you agree with the idea in exam-style Question 9. Then write down three key points to support your point of view.

Point 1: ....

Point 2: ....

Point 3: ....

2 Write down a piece of evidence to support each of the points in your answer to Question 1.

Evidence for point 1: ....

Evidence for point 2: ....

Evidence for point 3: ....

Evidence could be facts or statistics, an expert opinion or an example from your personal experience. The evidence you use in your writing in the exam does not have to be real or true, but it must be believable.

Guided

3 A counter-argument allows you to dismiss an opposing point of view. Think about the points you made in Question 1 above. What opposing points might somebody on the other side of the argument make? How could you dismiss them? Write down your ideas.

Some people might feel ....

....

....

However, ...

....

4 Rhetorical devices can strengthen your argument. Choose one of the following devices and use it to rewrite one sentence of your answer to Question 3.

rhetorical questions | direct address | repetition | lists | alliteration

contrast | pattern of three | emotive language | hyperbole

....

....

Writing for an audience

Some Paper 2 writing questions will clearly state the audience you should write for. Others may only imply or hint at the audience. Look at the exam-style question extract below. **You don't need to answer it**. Instead, think about how you might respond, then answer Questions 1 and 2.

Paper 2

9 Write an article for a national newspaper, exploring the idea that technology is taking over teenagers' lives. **(40 marks)**

Guided

1 Describe the implied audience for this piece of writing. Include your thoughts on age and gender.

The audience is likely to be ....

....

Remember to think about how wide the implied audience might be. For example, although their main audience might be adults, newspapers are read by people of all ages.

2 Which of the following sentences has the most appropriate tone and vocabulary for the audience you identified in Question 1? Circle your choice, then write a sentence to explain it.

A Some teenagers spend half their lives gawping at laptops and the telly, which I reckon is just such a waste of time.

B When you see a teenager staring at a computer, do not assume they are wasting their time.

....

....

Now look at this exam-style question. **You don't need to answer this question now**. Instead, think about the language you might use in your response, then answer Question 3.

Paper 2

8 Write a speech for Year 11 students at your school/college, encouraging them to take up a healthy lifestyle.

In your speech you could:

- describe what a healthy lifestyle involves, e.g. exercise, diet, avoiding drugs and alcohol
- give examples of the challenges of leading a healthy lifestyle and where to get help
- explain the benefits of adopting a healthy lifestyle

as well as any other ideas you might have. **(40 marks)**

Guided

3 An answer to Question 8 has been started for you below. Add two sentences to this opening.

Let's get straight to the point. The whole 'eat your five-a-day' routine is boring. Especially when your parents hammer it home on a daily basis, and particularly when it's followed by the inevitable 'don't be a couch potato' speech. We don't always want to hear what's good for us. However, if what you really want is clear skin and bags of energy, then increasing the amount of green vegetables you eat is a good starting point.

....

....

....

....

....

....

Had a go ☐ Nearly there ☐ Nailed it! ☐

Putting it into practice

Read the exam-style question below. **You don't need to answer this question**. Instead, think about how you might respond. Then answer Questions 1 and 2.

Paper 1

5 Write about a time when you, or someone you know, had to make an important decision. Your response could be real or imagined. **(40 marks)**

When you tackle this kind of question in the exam, remember to:
- plan your time – you have 45 minutes for this question, including planning and checking
- plan your writing, including ideas about narrative voice and language techniques
- make sure you write in prose
- make sure you stick to the same narrative voice throughout your writing.

1 Now plan the following:

Planning time: .... minutes

Writing time: .... minutes

Checking time:.................. minutes

Form: ....

Narrative voice: ....

2 Note down some ideas about language techniques you could use in your answer. Write a sentence giving an example of each technique.

Technique 1: ....

Example 1: ....

....

Technique 2: ....

Example 2: ....

....

Technique 3: ....

Example 3: ....

....

Technique 4: ....

Example 4: ....

....

Putting it into practice

Read the exam-style questions below. **You don't need to answer these questions**. Instead, think about what they are asking you to do, then complete the table.

Paper 2

8 Write a review of the facilities available at your local sports centre for a magazine.

In your review you could:

- describe the facilities that are available
- give details of opening times, costs and who the sports centre might appeal to
- give your opinion about the facilities that the sports centre offers

as well as any other ideas you might have. **(40 marks)**

Paper

9 Write an article for your local newspaper, exploring the idea that all dogs should be banned from your local park.

You could write about:

- who uses the park and what people use the park for, e.g. playground equipment for families, country paths for joggers
- how many dogs use the park and what the issues are at the moment
- the advantages/disadvantages of banning all dogs

as well as any other ideas you might have. **(40 marks)**

When you tackle these kinds of questions in the exam, remember to:

- plan your time – you have 45 minutes for this question, including planning and checking
- read the questions carefully and identify the topics
- annotate the question to highlight the form, audience and purpose
- plan your writing, including key features of the form and purpose

1 Plan a response to one of the exam-style questions above by completing this table.

	Question ___
Timing	Plan: minutes Write: minutes Check: minutes
Topic	
Form	
Audience	
Purpose	
Key features	

Had a go ☐ Nearly there ☐ Nailed it! ☐

Form: articles and reviews

Read the exam-style question below. **You don't need to answer this question**. Instead, think about what it is asking you to do, then answer Questions 1 to 3.

Paper 2

9 Write an article for your local newspaper, exploring the idea of a curfew of 9 pm in your home town, after which time all teenagers must return home.

You could write about:

- what teenagers do when out after 9 pm, e.g. visiting friends/family, cinema, sports clubs
- who might think teenagers are a problem after 9 pm, and why they might think this
- the advantages/disadvantages of making all teenagers return home by 9 pm

as well as any other ideas you might have. **(40 marks)**

1 Think of a title you could use as a headline for the piece of writing in Question 9.

....

....

....

Headlines use a range of techniques including: repetition, a rhetorical question, alliteration, a pun or a rhyme.

2 Think of a subheading that will add more information to your headline.

....

....

3 Articles often use quotations from experts to make the information seem factual and reliable. Who could you quote in this article? What would they say?

....

....

....

Like articles, reviews use headlines and subheadings, and inform the reader. However, some reviews also aim to entertain, so tend to use more figurative language than articles.

In the exam, you may be asked to write a review. Look at this exam-style question. **You don't need to answer this question now**. Instead, think about the language you might use in your response, then answer Question 4.

Paper 2

9 Write a review of your favourite TV programme for a local newspaper.

In your review you could:

- state when your programme is on and how often
- give examples of what makes your chosen programme so watchable
- share your ideas about why others should watch the programme, and give it a rating

as well as any other ideas you might have. **(40 marks)**

Guided

4 Write an opening paragraph for the review in Question 9, using figurative language to engage the reader. If you wish, use the opening that has been started for you below. It is about the television programme *I'm A Celebrity... Get Me Out Of Here!*

In the jungle, the skies darken, the heavens open and a talentless celebrity nobody has ever heard of chokes on a handful of live maggots. My favourite television programme is like

....

....

....

....

Form: letters and reports

Read this exam-style question. **You don't need to answer this question**. Instead, think about what you might need to include in your response, then answer Question 1.

Paper 2

8 Write a letter to your local television station, applying for a job as a news presenter.

In your letter you could:

- state why you are interested in the job
- describe the experience and skills that would make you an ideal candidate
- explain the benefits to the television station of employing you to present the news

as well as any other ideas you might have. **(40 marks)**

1 Decide whether the following statements are true or false. Circle your choices.

(a) You should make it clear that you are writing a letter, for example by using 'Dear…'. **True** **False**

(b) You should use 'Dear Sir/Madam' if you don't know the name of the person you are writing to. **True** **False**

(c) You should use 'Yours sincerely' if you have used 'Dear Sir/Madam'. **True** **False**

(d) You should use a formal subject line to draw attention to your topic. **True** **False**

If you are asked to write a letter in the exam, pay attention to the tone and content of your writing. You should also make it clear that you are writing a letter – for example, by using 'Dear…'.

Now read the following exam-style question. **You don't need to answer this question**. Instead, think about what might be needed for this piece of writing, then answer Questions 2 and 3.

Paper 2

9 Write a report for your local council, exploring the idea of setting up a youth council to give young people a voice.

You could write about:

- what a youth council could contribute, e.g. giving opinions on decisions being made about local services
- why young people might be keen to join a youth council
- how to encourage young people to become involved

as well as any other ideas you might have. **(40 marks)**

2 Reports need to be formal and factual. Write a headline and a suitable opening sentence for the report in Question 9 that give the main facts about the topic.

....

....

....

Guided

3 Reports are intended to inform their audience about a particular topic, and usually include recommendations. Look at the last bullet point in Question 9 above and suggest two recommendations you could use in your answer.

(a) Firstly, I would suggest ....

....

(b) ....

....

Form: information guides

Read this exam-style question. **You don't need to answer this question**. Instead, think about what you might need to include in your response, then answer Questions 1 to 4.

Paper 2

8 Write an information guide for a teenage visitor to your town or city.

In your guide you could:
- offer practical advice to help the teenagers find their way around
- include information about what there is to do and see
- explain where they can go to get further information

as well as any other ideas you might have. **(40 marks)**

1 Your information guide will need a heading or title to attract and engage the reader. Write down three possible headings for the guide in Question 8 using techniques such as alliteration, a pun or a pattern of three.

(a) ....

(b) ....

(c) ....

2 Choose the best of your headings in Question 1. Then explain why it would be the most effective for your teenage audience.

....

....

Guided

3 Subheadings help to structure an information text and guide the reader. Write down three subheadings that you could use in your information guide for teenagers. An example has been done for you.

(a) Sensational sports..........

(b) ....

(c) ....

4 Lists are a useful way to get across a large amount of information. They are often used at the start of an information guide to signpost to the reader what will be included in the guide. What could you list at the start of your information guide for teenagers? Write a list using no more than four bullet points.

....

....

....

....

....

....

Lists can be bulleted or numbered to show a sequence or ranking. Avoid using too many lists. You still need to show you can structure your writing to guide the reader, using sentences, paragraphs and adverbials. Go to page 71 to practise using adverbials.

Putting it into practice

Answer the exam-style question below. Focus in particular on audience, purpose and form.

Paper 2

8 Write a letter to the Prime Minister, suggesting improvements to the current education system.

In your letter you could:

- state what the current education system is like for students
- explain why changes should be made to the education system
- describe what needs improving about the current system, e.g. exams, school day timings, size of schools

as well as any other ideas you might have. **(40 marks)**

When you tackle this type of question in the exam, remember to:

- spend 45 minutes on your answer, including planning and checking time
- read the question carefully and identify the topic
- annotate the question to highlight the form, audience and purpose
- plan your writing before you start
- include all the relevant key features of the form and purpose.

Remember: You have more space than this to answer your question in the exam. Use your own paper to finish your answer to the question above.

Prose: an overview

For Paper 1, it is important that your imaginative writing takes an appropriate form.

1 Read the statements below about the writing questions that will appear on Paper 1. Decide whether each statement is true or false. Circle your choices.

(a) You should write in prose. **True** **False**

(b) You should not write a poem. **True** **False**

(c) You could write a play. **True** **False**

2 Look at the following list. For which of the options below is prose **not** the form usually used? Tick your choices.

(a) narratives (stories)

(b) descriptions

(c) poems

(d) monologues

3 Write a brief definition of prose.

....

....

4 Read the short extracts below. Identify which extract has clear features of narrative, description and monologue. Write the letters of the extracts in the spaces below.

Narrative (tip: look out for a sequence of events): ....

Description (tip: look out for a sense of place or person): ....

Monologue (tip: look out for a strong sense of voice): ....

A The gloom of the night was funereal; all nature seemed clothed in crape. The spiky points of the fir trees behind the house rose into the sky like the turrets and pinnacles of an abbey. Nothing below the horizon was visible save a light which was still burning in the cottage of Susan Nunsuch.

B You know, it still amazes me how so many people get out their flip flops at the first, barely visible hint of sun. Flip flops and barbeques. It's the appearance of the flip flops that I find most bewildering though. My feet, you see, are like little blocks of ice direct from the Arctic, even in July and August. I'm talking about the Arctic before global warming, too, in the days when it really was glacial.

C When I went into the room, my uncle was so contracted by the cold, and so huddled together in his chair behind the one dim candle, that I did not see him until I was close to the table.

As I held out my hand to him, he caught up his stick (being infirm, he always walked about the house with a stick), and made a blow at me, and said, "You fool!"

In the exam, make sure you structure your ideas carefully and for effect. Your writing should have a clear beginning, middle and end. Focus on full paragraphs and avoid too much dialogue.

Ideas and planning: imaginative

Read these exam-style questions. **You don't need to answer these questions**. Instead, consider the two question options, then answer Questions 1 to 3.

Paper 1

5 Write about a time when you, or someone you know, told a lie.
Your response could be real or imagined. **(40 marks)**

6 Look at images C and D on page 106.
Write about the trip of a lifetime.
Your response could be real or imagined. You may wish to base your response on one of the images. **(40 marks)**

1 In the exam, you will need to choose a title quickly to save time for detailed planning. Of the question options above, circle the one you have the most initial ideas about.

2 Write down your initial ideas for the option you chose in Question 1, either as a list or a spider diagram.

Try to picture the scene or event in your mind. (You can do this even if you have chosen Question 6 and are using the images.) Think about the characters (e.g. who is there, what they are like) and the action (e.g. what is happening, what has happened already).

Stay focused on the title you have chosen. After planning, quickly check that all your ideas are centred on this title.

Guided

3 Now look at a student's plan for Question 6, below. Add details to the plan, including ideas about imaginative writing techniques you could use.

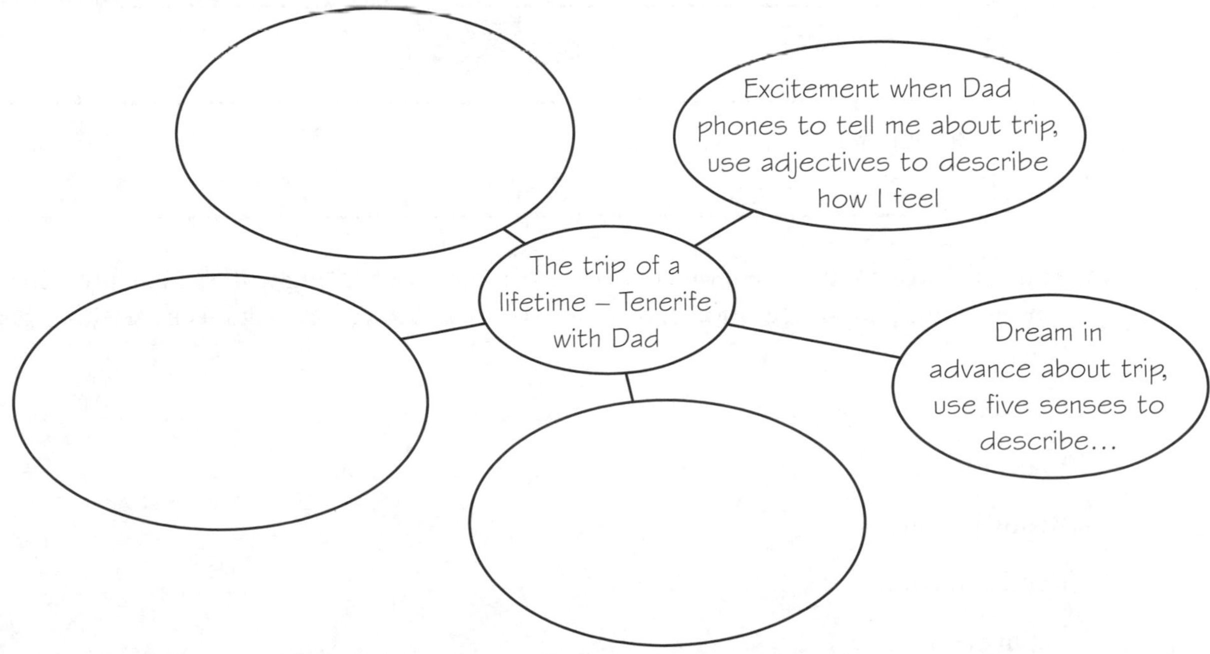

If you choose Question 6, you don't have to use the images provided. Go with whatever you feel will generate the most appropriate ideas. This student already had ideas about a trip so chose not to use the images.

Structure: imaginative

It is important to structure your imaginative writing effectively. The best way to achieve this is to use a narrative (story) structure. Look at this exam-style question. **You don't need to answer this question**. Instead, think about how you might structure an answer to this question, then answer Question 1 below.

Paper 1

5 Write about a time when you, or someone you know, met a long-lost relative or friend. Your response could be real or imagined. **(40 marks)**

Guided

1 Complete the narrative structure for a response to Question 5 below. Remember to include ideas about appropriate imaginative writing techniques in the plan.

Exposition: Relaxing in front of fire on windy winter day. Doorbell rings. I answer – it is my long-lost sister. Use dialogue...

Rising action: ....

Climax: ....

Falling action: ....

Resolution: ....

2 You can make a narrative more interesting, or tense, by playing with the narrative structure. Rewrite your plan in Question 1, this time starting at the climax and using flashbacks to tell the story.

Climax: ....

Exposition: ....

Rising action: ....

Return to climax: ....

Falling action: ....

Resolution: ....

Beginnings and endings: imaginative

The beginning of your imaginative writing needs to engage the reader immediately and set the tone for the rest of your writing.

Look at this exam-style question. **You don't need to answer this question now**. Instead, think about how you might begin and end an answer to this question, then answer Question 1 below.

Paper 1

5 Write about a time when you, or someone you know, discovered a secret. **(40 marks)**

Guided

1 Write several different beginnings in response to this exam-style question. One has been done for you.

Don't be tempted to over-use dialogue. Mix it in with plenty of prose, to demonstrate your sentence structure skills.

Vivid description	**Dialogue**
	"I'm telling you, I saw her out there, clear as day!" hissed my aunt. "Ssh" whispered my father. "Just keep the secret until she's old enough to handle it!" Through the tiny crack in the door I could see my father's anguished face. My mind raced ahead imagining a million different scenarios, none of them happy. Could they really be talking about my long-lost mother?
Mystery	**Conflict or danger**

The ending of a piece of imaginative prose is just as important as the opening. Choose one of your openings from Question 1, then answer Questions 2 and 3.

2 What will the tone of your ending be? Will it be happy, tense or sad? Write a sentence explaining how you would end your story.

....

....

3 Write three possible final sentences. Make sure you focus on creating the tone you decided on in Question 2.

(a) ....

(b) ....

(c) ....

Make your ending as imaginative as possible. Avoid clichés like 'and then I woke up and it was all a dream'.

Putting it into practice

Read the exam-style question below. **You don't need to answer this question**. Instead, think about what you could write about, then answer Question 1.

Paper 

5 Write about a time when you, or someone you know, stood up to a bully.
Your response could be real or imagined. **(40 marks)**

When you plan for this type of question in the exam, remember to:
- spend 10 minutes on a detailed plan
- plan for a clear narrative structure
- plan the narrative voice and imaginative writing techniques you will use.

1 Use the space below to plan your answer to the exam-style question above.

Ideas and planning: inform, explain, review

Read the exam-style question below. **You don't need to answer this question**. Instead, think about what it is asking you to do, then answer Question 1.

Paper 

8 Write a review of a mobile phone, or another technological device.

In your review you could:

- state what type of device you are reviewing and what functions it offers
- explain when and how it can be used, and who might find it useful
- describe how effective you think it is, and why

as well as any other ideas you might have. **(40 marks)**

Use the bullet points in the question to support your planning.

1 Plan an answer to Question 8. Work through the planning stages below and then complete the spider diagram. Some ideas have been added for you.

(a) Plan your introduction. Tell your reader what you are writing about and plan to be engaging so that they will want to read on.

(b) You will need three or four key points. Decide which key points you will include – use the bullet points in the question to guide you with this.

(c) Add detail to each of your key points, including techniques appropriate to your audience and purpose.

(d) Number your key points. Which will work best at the beginning and which at the end?

(e) Plan your conclusion.

(f) Add ideas for temporal adverbials that would help to guide your reader through your points.

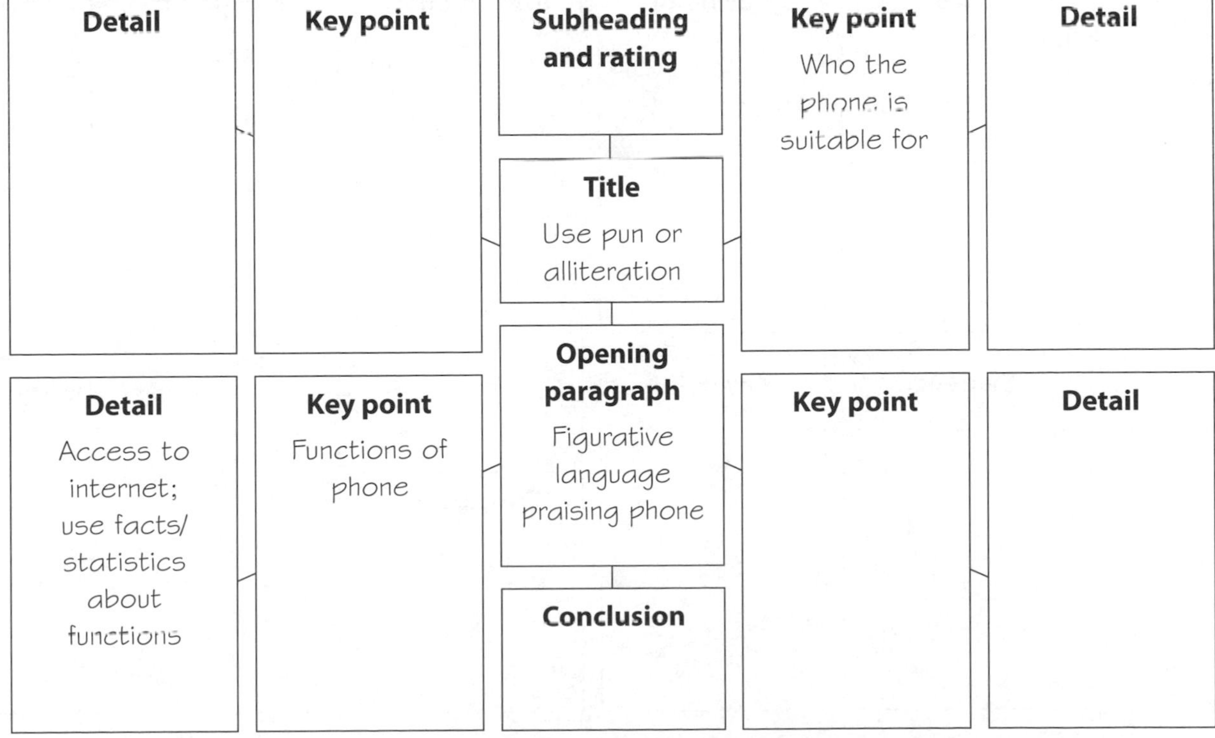

Plan your writing carefully. Quality is more important than quantity, so it is worth spending a whole 10 minutes on this stage.

Ideas and planning: argue and persuade

Read the exam-style question below. **You don't need to answer this question**. Instead, think about what it is asking you to do, then answer Question 1.

Paper 

9 Write an article for a magazine, exploring the value of exams in schools.

You could write about:

- the types of exams most students take, and how relevant they are
- the advantages and disadvantages of taking exams to test ability
- alternative ways to test students at the end of their schooling, e.g. coursework or practical tests

as well as any other ideas you might have. **(40 marks)**

1 Plan an answer to Question 9. Work through the planning stages and complete the spider diagram below.

(a) Summarise your response in the centre of the spider diagram below.

(b) To guide readers, plan an introduction that tells them what you are writing and why they should read it. Add it to the spider diagram.

(c) Decide on the **three** key points you will make.

(d) Decide on the evidence you will use to support your key points.

(e) Sequence your key points by numbering them. What would be the most logical or effective order?

(f) Add a counter-argument to your plan. What might someone who opposed your opinion argue? How can you dismiss their argument?

(g) Plan a conclusion that will reinforce your point of view.

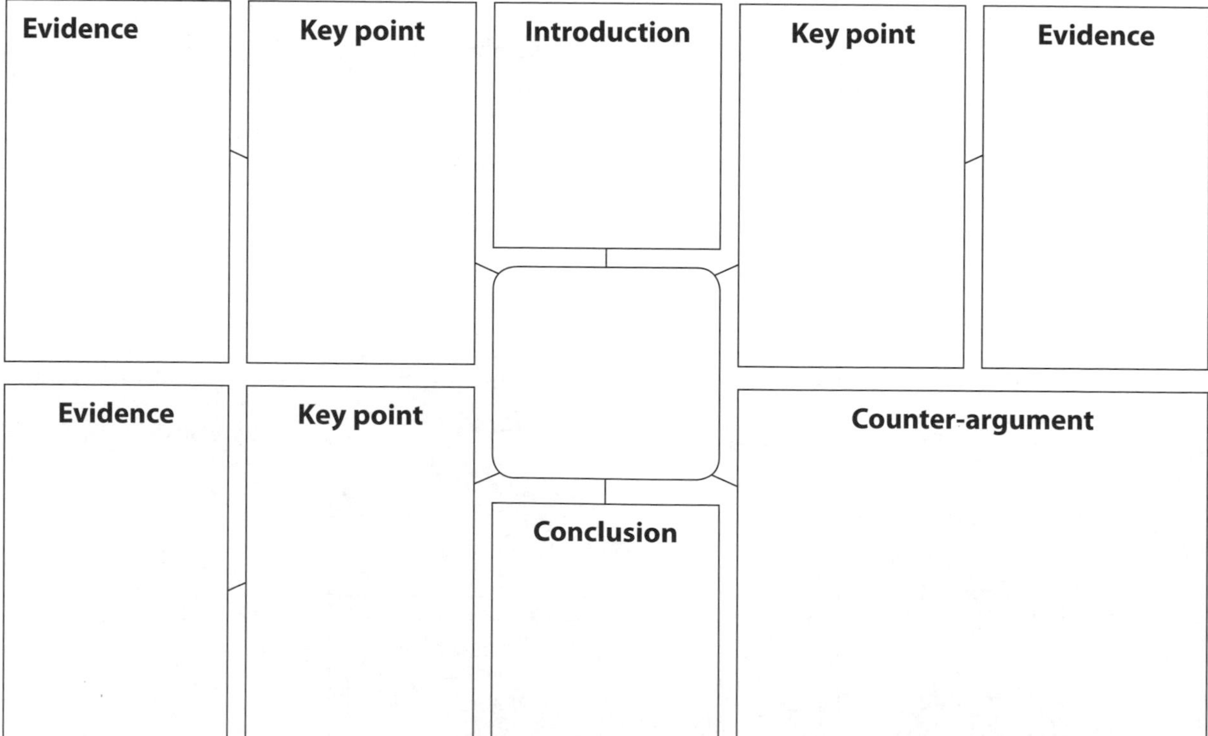

You only have 45 minutes to plan, write and check your answer – so aim for six paragraphs of well-crafted writing. Remember: quality is rewarded – quantity is not.

Openings: transactional

Read the exam-style question below. **You don't need to answer this question now**. Instead, think about what it is asking you to do, then answer Questions 1 and 2.

Paper 2

9 Write an article for a newspaper, exploring your ideas on whether prison prevents people from committing serious crimes.

You could write about:
- why prisons exist, what is their purpose and what crimes usually result in a prison sentence
- the alternatives to prison, e.g. community service or preventing people from leaving their homes
- the advantages and/or disadvantages of sending people to prison

as well as any other ideas you might have. **(40 marks)**

1 The first sentences of your writing must grab the readers' attention and make them want to read on. Try writing the opening sentence of your response to Question 9 in lots of different ways. An example has been done for you.

Using a rhetorical question: ....

....

Making a bold or controversial statement: ....

....

With a relevant quotation: ....

....

With a shocking or surprising fact or statistic: ....

....

With a short, relevant, **interesting** anecdote: My frail, elderly grandmother never recovered from a mugging. It happened in her own road, in broad daylight, in front of several dozen witnesses.

2 Choose one or two of your ideas from Question 1 and write the rest of your introduction to Question 9 above. Remember your opening paragraph needs to:
- introduce the topic you are writing about
- engage the reader.

....

....

....

....

....

....

....

Don't tell the reader what you are going to be writing in your article:

In this article I am going to argue that ... ✗

Just write it!

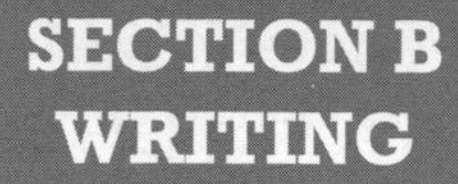

Had a go ☐ Nearly there ☐ Nailed it! ☐

Conclusions: transactional

Read the exam-style question below. **You don't need to answer this question now**. Instead, think about what it is asking you to do, then answer Questions 1 and 2.

Paper 2

9 Write an article for a newspaper, exploring your ideas on whether prison prevents people from committing serious crimes.

You could write about:

- why prisons exist, what is their purpose and what crimes usually result in a prison sentence
- the alternatives to prison, e.g. community service or preventing people from leaving their homes
- the advantages and/or disadvantages of sending people to prison

as well as any other ideas you might have. **(40 marks)**

Guided

1 The final paragraph or conclusion of your writing should make a lasting impression. Try writing sentences you could include in your conclusion to Question 9, using the techniques below. An example has been done for you.

End on a vivid image: ....

....

End on a warning: ....

....

End on a happy note: ....

....

End on a thought-provoking question: How many vulnerable old people will be violently assaulted?

End on a 'call to action': ....

....

Refer back to your introduction, but don't repeat it: ....

....

2 Choose one or two of your ideas from Question 1 and write your conclusion to Question 9 above.

....

....

....

....

....

....

....

....

....

....

Look back over your whole argument. Consider how you might sum it up to end your piece of writing neatly and leave your reader with a clear message.

Putting it into practice

Read the exam-style question below. **You don't need to answer this question**. Instead, think about what you are being asked to do, then answer Question 1.

Paper ②

8 Write a review for a magazine about an event you have attended in your local area.

In your review, you could write about:
- a film, concert, activity day, sports event, festival or any other local event
- what made the event particularly memorable
- who might enjoy this type of event, and why they would enjoy it

as well as any other ideas you might have. **(40 marks)**

When you plan for this type of question in the exam, remember to:
- read the question carefully and identify the topic
- identify the form, audience and purpose before you start
- spend about 10 minutes planning your answer
- plan the features and techniques you will use to support the form, audience and purpose
- organise and sequence your ideas
- plan your introduction and conclusion.

1 Use the space below to plan your answer to Question 8 above.

Had a go ☐ Nearly there ☐ Nailed it! ☐

Paragraphing for effect

Look at this exam-style question extract. You don't need to answer the exam-style question itself.

Paper 

9 Write an article for a newspaper, exploring the quality of careers advice available to students in schools. **(40 marks)**

Now look at the paragraph below. It is from a student's response to the exam-style question above.

> When students choose their GCSE options in Year Nine, they do not always choose subjects because they will help them in their future career. I chose my GCSEs either because I liked the teacher or because lots of my friends had chosen that subject. Neither of these reasons is sound. With more advice on the careers available to us and the different ways we can prepare for them, students would make more informed and more sensible decisions.

This student has organised the paragraphs in her argument using Point–Evidence–Explain.

1 Identify and label the three different sections of this paragraph: point, evidence and explain.

2 Plan your own Point–Evidence–Explain paragraph in answer to Question 9 above.

Point: ....

Evidence: ....

Explain: ....

3 Now write the paragraph you have planned in full.

....

....

....

....

....

....

....

....

....

4 Identify and label the three different sections of your paragraph: **point**, **evidence** and **explain**.

Each time you start a new point, start a new paragraph. If you are writing to inform, explain or describe, start each paragraph with a topic sentence.

Linking ideas

Different adverbials have different purposes.

1 Copy the adverbials below into the table, adding each one to the correct column.

Consequently	Furthermore	In particular	Significantly
For example	However	In the same way	Similarly
For instance	On the other hand	Moreover	Therefore

Adding an idea	Explaining	Illustrating	Emphasising	Comparing	Contrasting
		For example			

Remember that time or temporal adverbials – such as afterwards, before, meanwhile – are very useful for indicating the passage of time in imaginative writing.

Read the exam-style question below. **You don't need to answer this question now**. Instead, think about what it is asking you to do, then answer Questions 2 and 3.

Paper 2

9 Write an article for a magazine, exploring the value of exams in schools.

You could write about:

- the types of exams most students take, and how relevant they are
- the advantages and disadvantages of taking exams to test ability
- alternative ways to test students at the end of their schooling, e.g. coursework or practical tests

as well as any other ideas you might have. **(40 marks)**

2 Look at the paragraphs below. They are extracts from one student's response to Question 9. Fill in all of the gaps using appropriate adverbials.

Many students are enormously successful in areas which exams do not or cannot assess. ...., one student at my school runs his own business designing websites for local companies. This is not something he has learned at school and .... his success will not be reflected in his exam results.

........................, some students' success depends not on hard work but on natural ability. .... this has more impact on less academic students. One student, ..., might achieve an A grade with little or no hard work, while another might have worked solidly and consistently for years to achieve a 'C'.

3 Now write your own Point–Evidence–Explain paragraph in response to Question 9 above. Remember to use a range of adverbials to guide the reader through your argument.

Look back at your planning on page 66 to help you.

....

....

....

....

....

Putting it into practice

Answer the exam-style question below. Focus in particular on your use of paragraphs and adverbials.

Paper 2

9 Write an article for a magazine, exploring a great invention or discovery.

You could write about:

- any invention that has changed life for mankind, e.g. electricity, the telephone, the internet, the wheel, penicillin
- how the invention or discovery works and what it does
- who has benefitted from the invention or discovery.

as well as any other ideas you might have.

(40 marks)

When you tackle any writing question in the exam, remember to:

- write in paragraphs
- plan one main point or idea per paragraph
- use P-E-E to structure your paragraphs
- organise and sequence your paragraphs
- use adverbials to link your paragraphs and guide your reader through your ideas.

Remember: You have more space than this to answer your question in the exam. Use your own paper to finish your answer to the question above.

Vocabulary for effect: synonyms

Synonyms are words with similar meanings. You can use them to avoid repetition and to add variety to your writing.

1 Look at the sentence below. Think of **at least two** synonyms for each circled word.

Synonyms for 'students':

1 ....

2 ....

3 ....

Synonyms for 'improve':

1 ....

2 ....

3 ....

Students can improve their learning by doing more revision.

Synonyms for 'learning':

1 ....

2 ....

3 ....

Synonyms for 'doing':

1 ....

2 ....

3 ....

If you get stuck, use a thesaurus – but first TRY to use the large vocabulary that you already have in your head. Remember, you won't have access to a thesaurus in the exam.

Guided

2 Look at each of the words in the table below. Complete the table by adding at least two synonyms for each word. An example has been done for you.

embarrassed	upset	scream	moment	annoyed
humiliated ashamed mortified				

Look at the exam-style question below. You don't need to answer the exam-style question itself. Think about what you might include in a response to this question, then answer Question 3.

Paper 1

5 Write about a time when you, or someone you know, felt embarrassed.
Your response could be real or imagined. **(40 marks)**

3 Write a paragraph in response to the exam-style question above. Use some of your vocabulary from Question 2 in your writing.

....

....

....

....

....

....

Had a go ☐ Nearly there ☐ Nailed it! ☐

Vocabulary for effect: argue and persuade

Emotive words are important when you are writing to argue or persuade.

Guided

1 Look at the sentences below. Rewrite them, using emotive language to add more impact. The first example has been done for you.

A Animals in laboratories are frequently treated really badly and then put to sleep.

Animals in laboratories are frequently treated cruelly and then slaughtered.

B If we continue to use too many of the earth's resources, the world will not have enough food.

....

....

C Our lives are filled with computers. We may not like it but we cannot do much about it.

....

....

2 Look at this sentence:

Some parents greeted the school's controversial plans with a (cry) of disapproval.

What would be the impact of replacing the circled word with

(a) roar : ....

(b) howl : ....

(c) whimper : ....

Look at the exam-style question extract below. **You don't need to answer this question now**. Instead, think about what you might include in a response to this question, then answer Question 3.

Paper

9 Write an article for a community newspaper, exploring the idea that social networking is a waste of time. **(40 marks)**

3 Write two sentences in response to Question 9 above. Aim to choose vocabulary for its impact and its connotations.

....

....

....

....

....

Language for different effects 1

You can add power and impact to your writing by using a range of language techniques.

Guided

1 Look at the extracts from students' writing below. Some are taken from a piece of imaginative writing, some from a piece of transactional writing. Connect the rhetorical techniques to the extracts. An example has been done for you.

A
Why was he staring at me like that?

B
I stared at the crowd in front of me: thin people, fat people, tall people, short people, old people, young people. I recognised none of them.

C
Some people carefully sort their rubbish into recycling bins, separating their metal, card, paper, plastic and glass. Most people just chuck it all in one big bin.

Contrast

Rhetorical question

Repetition

List

D
As the phone rang, the bright sunshine disappeared, swallowed by a wall of rolling dark clouds.

E
How would you feel if it were your beloved dog or cat being treated in this way?

F
The only solution which we should consider, the only solution which the human race can offer, the only solution which we can all contribute to, is right under our noses.

Now look at the exam-style question below. **You don't need to answer this question now**. Instead, think about the language techniques you might use in a response, then answer Question 2.

Paper 2

8 Write a letter to your local pet shop, expressing your views about keeping small animals in cages.

In your letter you could:

- state why you are writing
- describe what animals they have in cages and what life is like for those animals
- explain the advantages and disadvantages of keeping the animals in cages

as well as any other ideas you might have. **(40 marks)**

2 Write up to four short extracts from an answer to Question 8 above. Use one or more of the language techniques explored in Question 1 in each extract.

....

....

....

....

....

....

....

....

Had a go ☐ Nearly there ☐ Nailed it! ☐

Language for different effects 2

You can add power and impact to your writing by using a range of language techniques.

1 Look at the extracts from students' writing below. Some are taken from a piece of imaginative writing, some from a piece of transactional writing. Connect the rhetorical techniques to the extracts in which they are used.

A
For about the hundredth time that day, my sister started sobbing.

B
How would you feel if it were your beloved dog or cat being treated in this way?

C
The city stretched before me, dark, dangerous and disturbing.

Direct address

Pattern of three

Alliteration

Hyperbole

D
This is an appalling waste of money. We might as well be setting light to wads of ten pound notes and laughing as we do it.

E
We must act intelligently, decisively and immediately.

F
Don't just sit there! Get off the sofa and do something.

Now look at the exam-style question below. **You don't need to answer this question now**. Instead, think about the language techniques you might use in a response, then answer Question 2.

Paper

8 Your local newspaper is holding a speech writing competition and entries are invited under the heading 'School is cruel'. Write a speech as your competition entry.

In your speech you could:

- give examples of ways in which school might be considered 'cruel'
- describe who might find school cruel and why
- explain your ideas about whether school is cruel and whether schools should be changed

as well as any other ideas you might have. **(40 marks)**

2 Write up to four short extracts from an answer to Question 8 above. Use one or more of the language techniques explored in Question 1 in each extract.

Language for different effects 3

Figurative language can be used to create powerful images in the mind of a reader.

Guided

1 Look at the examples of figurative language used in the sentences below. The writers have used similes, metaphors and personification to give their writing impact. But which sentence uses which technique? Circle the correct answer.

	Sentence			
A	The wind sang in the trees and the branches waved.	simile	metaphor	personification
B	The school has a challenging task ahead – an Everest to be climbed.	simile	metaphor	personification
C	She smiled like a tiger, licking its lips at the sight of a lost child.	simile	metaphor	personification
D	Waiting for the exams to begin is like waiting on death row.	(simile)	metaphor	personification
E	Homework is a ball and chain around every students' ankle.	simile	metaphor	personification
F	It's at that moment that your completely empty revision timetable creeps up behind you, taps you on the shoulder and asks if it could 'have a word'.	simile	metaphor	personification

Now look at the exam-style question below. **You don't need to answer this question now.** Instead, think about the figurative language you might use in a response, then answer Question 2.

Paper 1

5 Write about a time when you, or someone you know, found something hidden.
Your response can be real or imagined. **(40 marks)**

2 Write up to four short extracts from an answer to Question 5 above. Use one of the figurative devices explored in Question 1 in each extract.

....

....

....

....

....

Don't try to use one simile, one metaphor and one example of personification in your answers. Do look for opportunities where they will add impact to your ideas. Do avoid clichés and be original.

Had a go ☐ Nearly there ☐ Nailed it! ☐

Using the senses

Look at the examples of descriptive language used in the extracts below. The writer has used the five senses in an effort to engage the reader and make the descriptions more vivid.

A Strange aromas wafted in through the vents in the basement wall...

B Dusty wooden floorboards creaked in time to my footsteps...

C I could see the smoke wafting from the chimney of the empty house...

D Bitter juices filled my mouth as my hand brushed against...

E A large, red, crispy looking pizza was fresh from the oven. It lay in a pan on the hob, sizzling and dripping its aromatic juices.

1 Circle the two extracts that you feel are particularly effective.

> Try to avoid starting sentences with phrases such as 'I could smell...' or 'I saw...'. Imaginative writing is far more effective if you 'show' rather than 'tell' the reader.

2 Why are the two examples you have selected so effective? Write one sentence explaining how each example engages the reader.

Example 1 ....

....

Example 2 ....

....

Look at the exam-style question title below. **You don't need to answer this question now**. Instead, think about what you might include in a response to this title, then answer Question 3.

Paper ①

> **5** Write about a time when you, or someone you know, felt afraid.
> Your response could be real or imagined. **(40 marks)**

3 Write the opening paragraph of a response to this exam-style question. Try to:

- use at least three of the five senses
- include examples of figurative language such as similes, metaphors and personification.

....

....

....

....

....

....

....

Narrative voice

Look at the narrative extracts below, then answer Question 1.

A	In the end it didn't matter. I lost the game all on my own that day.	first person	third person	omniscient third person
B	She had expected somebody tall, dark and handsome. He had hoped for somebody short and cuddly. As she looked down, he reached up to shake her slender, bony hand. They both realised that if the date was to work, they would need to learn the art of compromise.	first person	third person	omniscient third person (circled)
C	To be honest it was all a huge fuss and about practically nothing. It wasn't as if I had actually killed anybody.	first person	third person	omniscient third person
D	Sheila seemed to have no conscience; she seemed to positively enjoy seeing other people in pain. Tears ran down Carol's face in great streaks but Sheila's only concern was the queue for a taxi. They were going to be very late unless the girl pulled herself together very quickly.	first person	third person	omniscient third person

Guided

1 For each extract above, identify the narrative voice. Circle the correct answers. An example has been done for you.

Look at the exam-style question below. **You don't need to answer this question now**. Instead, think about how you might open a response to this title, then answer Question 2.

Paper 1

5 Write about a time when you, or someone you know, took a stand about something. Your response could be real or imagined. **(40 marks)**

2 Write two possible openings of a response to this exam-style question. Aim to write one or two sentences for each opening. Use a different narrative voice in each opening.

Remember:

- Always check whether the question tells you which narrative voice to use.
- An omniscient third person narrator can see into any character's mind.
- If you want to allow your reader to feel very close to your main character, use first person narration.

(a) ....

....

(b) ....

....

Putting it into practice

Answer the exam-style question below. Focus in particular on your use of language and language techniques for effect.

Paper 2

8 Write a letter to a well-known celebrity, asking them to appear at a fundraising event for your favourite charity.

In your letter you could:

- state why you are writing and give details about the charity
- describe what you want them to do at the charity event
- explain why you think the celebrity might want to get involved

as well as any other ideas you might have. **(40 marks)**

When you tackle any writing question in the exam, you should think about language. Remember to:

- annotate the question to highlight the form, audience and purpose
- choose language that is appropriate for the audience and purpose
- choose language techniques with care and for impact
- avoid using too many techniques – it is more important that your writing is well structured and appropriate for the audience and purpose.

Remember: You have more space than this to answer your question in the exam. Use your own paper to finish your answer to the question above.

Putting it into practice

Write a response to the exam-style question below. Focus in particular on your use of language and language techniques for effect.

Paper 1

5 Write about a time when you, or someone you know, found a locked room.
Your response could be real or imagined. **(40 marks)**

When you tackle any writing question in the exam, you should think about language. Remember to:

- choose language that is appropriate to your audience
- make ambitious and effective vocabulary choices to engage your reader
- use a range of language techniques
- avoid using too many examples of simile, metaphor or personification – a few original ideas are far more effective than a mass of clichés.

Remember: You have more space than this to answer your question in the exam. Use your own paper to finish your answer to the question above.

Had a go ☐ Nearly there ☐ Nailed it! ☐

Sentence variety 1

Using a range of different sentence types can help you to convey your ideas clearly and engage your reader.

Guided

1 Look at the sentences below and identify the sentence type. Are they:

A a single-clause sentence
B a multi-clause sentence with a subordinate clause
C a multi-clause sentence with a coordinate clause
D a multi-clause sentence with a relative clause
E a minor sentence?

For each one, identify the sentence type by writing a letter in the space. Then write a sentence to explain how you know. One has been done for you.

(a) We must act now because soon it may be too late.
Type: .... Explanation:..

(b) Surely not.
Type: .... Explanation:..

(c) I hurried but I was too late.
Type: .... Explanation:..

(d) He gave her an apple.
Type: A Explanation: It has only one clause, with just one verb.

(e) The bus, which should have been there at half past ten, failed to arrive.
Type: .... Explanation:..

Look at the exam-style question extract below. **You don't need to answer this question now**. First, think how you might use different sentence types in a response.

Paper

9 Write an article for a national newspaper, exploring the idea that sportsmen and women are poor role models for young people. **(40 marks)**

Now consider this extract from one student's answer to Question 9, then answer Question 2.

Professional footballers are possibly the worst 'fakers'. With just one tap from another player they fall over. Sometimes they dive to the ground. Occasionally they fly. They always start screaming. It shows they are seriously injured. They say it was a foul. They demand a free kick. It is ridiculous.

2 The extract from the student's answer uses mainly short, single-clause sentences. Rewrite the extract. Aim to use a variety of the different sentence types.

....

....

....

....

....

Sentence variety 2

Look at the exam-style question title below. **You don't need to answer this question now**. Instead, think about what you might include in a response, then answer Questions 1 and 2.

Paper 1

5 Write about a time when you, or someone you know, moved to a big city.
Your response could be real or imagined. **(40 marks)**

Guided

1 Write a sentence that you could use in your answer to the above exam-style question, beginning with the following. An example has been done for you.

(a) a pronoun (e.g. I, he, she, they): I grew up in a tiny village in the middle of nowhere.

(b) an article (e.g. a, an, the): ....

(c) a preposition (e.g. above, behind, between): ....

(d) an -ing word (or present participle) (e.g. running, hurrying, crawling): ....

(e) an adjective (e.g. slow, quiet, violent): ....

(f) an adverb (e.g. alarmingly, painfully, happily): ....

(g) a conjunctive (subordinate clause + main clause) (e.g. if, although, because): ....

Think about the first word of your sentences. Varying the first word adds interest to your writing.

2 Now write a paragraph in response to the above exam-style question. Aim to use:

- all seven different types of sentence opener in your writing
- a different word to start each of your sentences.

....

Sentences for different effects

The ladder tipped over, the paint pot went flying, the paint exploded over her sofa, the paint pot hit her treasured vase, and the vase smashed into dust. I froze.

1 In the example above, a long, multi-clause sentence is followed by a short, single-clause sentence. What effect is this intended to have on the reader?

....

....

Guided 2 In the sentences below the same ideas have been used, but in a different order.

A Before I walked the six miles home, I scrubbed every last drop of paint from the carpet and swept up every last crumb of glass, while she watched with a grim smile of quiet satisfaction on her lips.

B While she watched with a grim smile of quiet satisfaction on her lips, I scrubbed every last drop of paint from the carpet and swept up every last crumb of glass before I walked the six miles home.

How does the order in which the information is organised affect each sentence's emphasis?

The first sentence emphasises ....

....

....

....

Look at the exam-style question extract below. **You don't need to answer this question now**. Instead, think about how you might begin an answer, then answer Question 3.

Paper 2

8 Write a speech for a Year 11 assembly, encouraging students to raise funds for the charity Children in Need. **(40 marks)**

Avoid overloading a sentence with too much information spread over a number of subordinate clauses. This can cause the reader to lose attention.

3 Write the opening two or three sentences of your own response to Question 8 above. Aim to include a:

- long, multi-clause sentence followed by a short, single-clause sentence
- sentence structured to give specific emphasis.

....

....

....

....

....

....

....

Putting it into practice

Answer the exam-style question below. Focus in particular on varying your sentences for effect.

Paper 2

9 Write an article for a newspaper, exploring the idea that sugary drinks and snacks should be banned in schools.

You could write about:

- what types of sugary drinks and snacks are brought into school
- why young people enjoy such drinks and snacks
- the advantages/disadvantages of banning sugary drinks and snacks

as well as any other ideas you might have. **(40 marks)**

When you tackle any writing question in the exam, you should think about sentence variety. Remember to:

- use a range of sentence types
- start your sentences in a range of different ways
- structure your sentences for effect
- avoid overloading individual sentences with too much information.

Remember: You have more space than this to answer your question in the exam. Use your own paper to finish your answer to the question above.

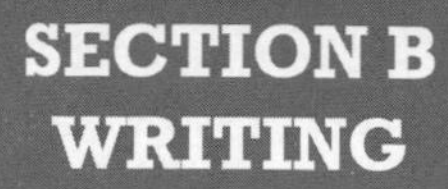

Ending a sentence

Failing to use full stops, question marks, exclamation marks and capital letters correctly affects the quality of your writing.

1 When should you use a full stop? ....

2 When should you use a question mark? ....

Guided

3 What three mistakes should you avoid when using exclamation marks? An example has been done for you.

(a) You should avoid scattering exclamation marks randomly throughout your writing, and instead use them sparingly.

(b) ....

(c) ....

4 Look at the sentences below. Tick the two sentences that are punctuated correctly. Cross the one that is not.

A I knew that what she had done was wrong, I had to persuade her to do something about it.

B I knew that what she had done was wrong. I had to persuade her to do something about it.

C I knew that what she had done was wrong and I had to persuade her to do something about it.

> You do not use a comma to join two pieces of information in a sentence. Use a full stop to separate them or a conjunction to join them. So check every time you use a comma: should it be a comma or is the sentence complete?

Now write a sentence explaining your decision. ....

5 Look at this student's writing. Correct all the full stop, question mark and exclamation mark errors you can find.

A Change of Heart!!

I braced myself for a confrontation, she was looking at me like she knew I had something to say and she didn't want to hear it. My heart began to race and a strange throbbing pain pulsed in my forehead. How could I say it. How could I tell her what I was thinking without upsetting her.

She knew something was coming, tears were welling up in her dark brown eyes and her bottom lip was starting to quiver. I didn't feel much better than she did, my stomach was churning and I could feel my legs shaking. I tried to speak, my mouth felt like sandpaper, it was dry and rough and I couldn't form the words.

Commas

If you are confident with using commas, you will write more effective multi-clause sentences and lists.

Guided

1 Look at the sentences below. Some have used commas correctly. Some have not. Tick the correct sentences and cross the incorrect ones. Two examples have been done for you.

Commas in lists

☒ **A** They can comfort, us in a crisis help out when we're in trouble make us laugh or make us cry.

☐ **B** It doesn't matter whether they're tall, short, thin, fat, heart-stoppingly attractive or mirror-crackingly ugly.

☐ **C** She was loud, angry, obnoxious and painfully honest.

Commas in multi-clause sentences with subordinate clauses

☑ **D** Whether we like it or not, friends can hurt as well as help us.

☐ **E** Friends can hurt as well as help us whether we like it or not.

☐ **F** Although I had known her since primary school we never spoke again.

Commas in multi-clause sentences with relative clauses

☐ **G** The problem which we may not want to face, is that friends can sometimes let us down.

☐ **H** A friend who I will not name once told me all my worst faults.

☐ **I** Her house, which I only ever visited once, was enormous.

2 Look again at all the sentences in Question 1. Correct any that you marked as incorrect.

Look at the exam-style question below. **You don't need to answer this question now**. Instead, think about what you might include in a response, then answer Question 3.

Paper 1

5 Write about a time when you, or someone you know, felt envious.
Your response could be real or imagined. **(40 marks)**

Remember to end your sentences correctly. Avoid using a comma splice.

3 Write three to five sentences in response to the exam-style question above. Use commas correctly to separate:

- items in a list
- a main and subordinate clause
- a main and relative clause.

....

....

....

....

....

....

Apostrophes and speech punctuation

Make sure you know how to avoid the common errors of missing out or using incorrect apostrophes and speech punctuation.

1 Look at the sentences below. Some have used apostrophes correctly. Some have not. Tick the correct sentences and cross the incorrect ones.

Apostrophes in contractions

☐ **A** I do'nt see her very often.

☐ **B** I can't believe how things turned out.

☐ **C** She wouldnt answer the phone.

Apostrophes of possession

☐ **D** My teachers' face was a picture.

☐ **E** The school's reaction was incredible.

☐ **F** The boys' faces all lit up.

Speech punctuation

☐ **G** 'I don't believe it!' she shouted.

☐ **H** 'Never mind.'

☐ **I** 'Come over here.' he whispered.

2 Look again at all the sentences in Question 1. Correct any that you marked as incorrect.

Guided 3 Now write a conversation between two friends in which they discuss a boy whose behaviour has resulted in several teachers ringing his parents. Aim to use apostrophes and speech marks correctly.

'Hey,' she called. 'Come over here.'

'What do you want?' I asked. ....

....

....

....

....

....

....

....

....

Remember:
- apostrophes in contractions are used to replace **missing letters**
- apostrophes of possession are always placed **at the end of the noun** whether it's plural (teachers') or singular (teacher's)
- in dialogue, there is always a punctuation mark **before** the closing speech marks.

Colons, semi-colons, dashes, brackets and ellipses

Punctuation helps you to express yourself clearly. It can also help you to develop your ideas.

1 Look at the sentences below. How could you alter or add to the punctuation, using a colon or a semi-colon?

Colons and semi-colons

A There is only one thing you can do to improve your grades. Revise.

B Teachers can help. They can give revision tips and answer any questions you have about the exam.

C Revision isn't easy. It takes time and willpower.

D Exams are the problem. Revision is the solution.

> You can use a semi-colon to link two connected ideas instead of using a conjunction. You can use a colon to introduce:
> - a list
> - an example
> - an explanation.

Dashes and brackets

Guided

2 Look at the sentences below. Some have used dashes and brackets correctly. Some have not. Tick the correct sentences and cross the incorrect ones. An example has been done for you.

☐ A My revision – which mainly involves staring into space – began this morning.

☐ B A short break (or sometimes a long break) helps clear your mind and recharge your battery.

☐ C My bedroom walls are covered in scribbled revision notes and key points (not a pretty sight.

☑ D Sometimes I wonder why I bother – and then I remember.

3 Look again at all the sentences in Question 2. Correct any that you marked as incorrect.

Look at the exam-style question below. **You don't need to answer this question now**. Instead, think about what you might include in a response, then answer Question 4.

Paper 1

> **5** Write about a time when you, or someone you know, overcame a personal challenge. Your response could be real or imagined. **(40 marks)**

4 Write three to five sentences in response to the exam-style question above. Try to use:
- a colon and a semi-colon
- dashes, brackets and an ellipsis.

....

....

....

....

....

....

....

....

....

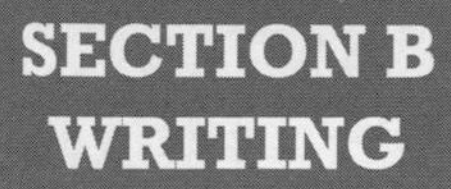

Had a go ☐ Nearly there ☐ Nailed it! ☐

Putting it into practice

Answer the exam-style question below. Focus in particular on punctuation.

Paper 2

8 Write a letter to your Headteacher/Principal, applying for a job as a part-time student receptionist at your school.

In your letter you could:

- state why you are interested in the position
- describe the experience and skills that make you an ideal candidate
- explain what both you and the school could gain if you get the job

as well as any other ideas you might have. **(40 marks)**

When you tackle any writing question in the exam, you should think about punctuation. Remember to:

- use a range of punctuation accurately, including advanced punctuation such as colons and semi-colons
- plan your time carefully so that you have time to check the accuracy of your punctuation.

Remember: You have more space than this to answer your question in the exam. Use your own paper to finish your answer to the question above.

Common spelling errors 1

Some of the most common spelling errors in students' writing are a result of misusing or confusing the following:

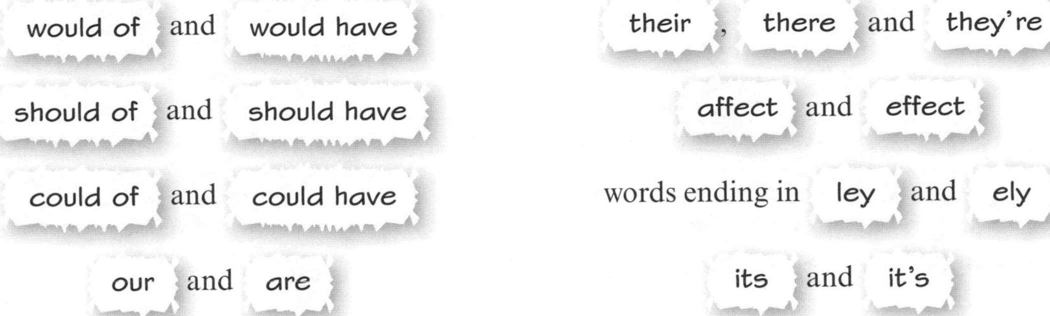

would of and would have
should of and should have
could of and could have
our and are
their, there and they're
affect and effect
words ending in ley and ely
its and it's

1 Identify and correct any spelling errors in these sentences.

A They went all the way back to there house.

B It would of been absolutley unbelievable – if I hadn't seen it with my own eyes.

C One affect of this issue is extremley concerning.

D Their first problem was how to get the students interested.

E Their our three reasons for this.

F There refusing to do anything about it.

G The school offered it's help immediately.

H We felt that students should definitley of been involved.

I Its not only the teachers who our effected by this situation.

J We were forced to reconsider are plan.

K It could not of been achieved without there help.

L Many students felt it had affected them negativley.

M Its not the first time this has happened.

- There are very few words ending in **ley**.
- **Would of**, **could of** and **should of** are **always** incorrect.

Had a go ☐ Nearly there ☐ Nailed it! ☐

Common spelling errors 2

Some of the most common spelling errors in students' writing are a result of misusing or confusing the following:

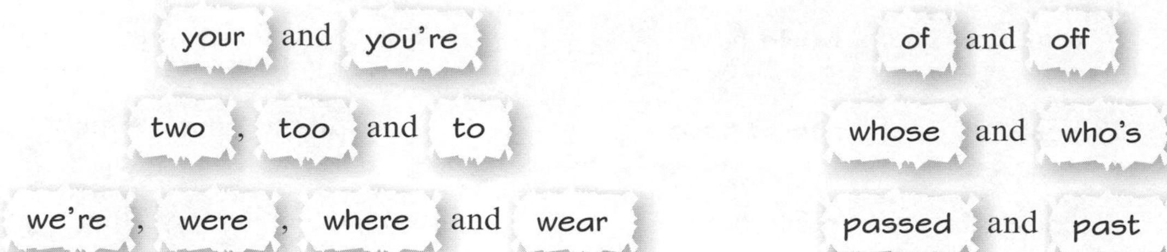

1 Identify and correct any spelling errors in these sentences:

A He did not know were he was going or who's idea it was.

B To many people make the same mistake.

C The time for worrying has past.

D This has taken some of the pressure of us.

E Your never sure whether you're doing enough to help.

F Whose going to complain about that?

G We where the first people there but still they ignored us.

H They walked passed us as though we wear invisible.

I They went too far, taking it too an extreme.

J How can we tell who's to blame?

K It can be difficult to know when your in the wrong.

L Support for the idea soon began to fall of.

M We simply don't know whose argument to believe and whether were expected to agree or not.

Remember:
A lot is two words. '**Alot** of people make this mistake' is wrong, but '**A lot** of people make this mistake' is correct.

Common spelling errors 3

Some of the most frequently misspelt words are explored in the table below. Make sure you learn how to spell these words properly.

argument	arguement	argumant
dificult	difficult	diffacult
disappoint	dissappoint	disapoint
disappear	dissappear	disapear
embarrassing	embarassing	embarasing
possesion	possession	posession
beggining	begining	beginning
recomend	recommend	reccomend
occassionaly	ocasionally	occasionally
definately	definitely	definitley
separately	seperately	seperatley
conscious	conshus	concsous
conshence	conscience	concsience
experiance	experance	experience
indapendance	independence	independance
beleive	believe	beleve
weird	wierd	weerd
business	busness	buisness
rythm	rhytm	rhythm
decision	desicion	desision
greatfull	grateful	greatful

1 Look carefully at the words in the table. In each row, one spelling is correct and two are incorrect. Tick the correct spelling and cross out the incorrect spellings.

> Correct spelling **can be learned**. Every time you spell a word incorrectly, make a note of the word and start to practise the correct spelling on a regular basis. Try strategies like looking for a hidden word within the word you are learning to spell, or saying what you see.

2 Now check your answers on page 128. Use the space below to write any spellings from the table above that you are unsure of. Practise them on a regular basis.

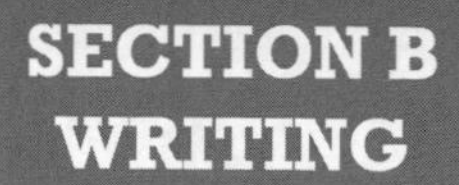

Had a go ☐ Nearly there ☐ Nailed it! ☐

Proofreading

Proofreading is important. In the exam, plan your time carefully so you have time to check your work for errors.

1 Look at the extract from one student's writing below. Read it carefully, looking for any:

- spelling errors
- punctuation errors
- grammatical errors – e.g. misused, repeated or missing words.

Circle and correct all the errors you can find.

> Scotland is the most amazing place Ive ever visited, even though it took ten hours to drive there it was worth it the moment i saw were we were staying. Huge blue lochs, rolling green hills, miles and miles of pine forest. They even looked beautiful driving passed them in a a car.
>
> On the first day we took the dogs for a long walk through a forest, it was the quitest place Ive ever been. Even with my brother their, all you could hear was the sound of leafs rustling in the breeze, the birds singing and you're heart beating.
>
> Are hotel was great, the scottish people are so frendly. I would definitley stay there again.

2 Look back at three or four pieces of writing you have completed recently. How many errors can you find? In the table below, note down words which you have misspelt and the **kinds** of punctuation and grammatical errors you have made.

Spelling errors	Punctuation errors	Grammatical errors

Train your proofreading brain to look out for the kinds of punctuation and grammatical errors you are prone to making. When the alarm rings, **stop!** Double check and correct any mistakes.

3 Use the space below to practise and learn all the spellings you have noted in the table.

Putting it into practice

Answer the exam-style question below. Focus in particular on proofreading your answer.

Paper 2

9 Write a report for your Headteacher/Principal, exploring the pressures teenagers like yourself face.

You could write about:

- the different kinds of pressure young people are under
- the ways young people respond to the pressures
- your ideas about how the school/college could help to reduce some of these pressures

as well as any other ideas you might have. **(40 marks)**

When you tackle any writing question in the exam, remember to:

- save time after you have finished writing to check the accuracy of your writing
- look out for the spelling, punctuation and grammatical errors that you know you tend to make.

Remember: You have more space than this to answer your question in the exam. Use your own paper to finish your answer to the question above.

Cut along the dotted lines and staple the texts together to make your own handy anthology. Make sure you keep it safe with your Workbook.

Text 1

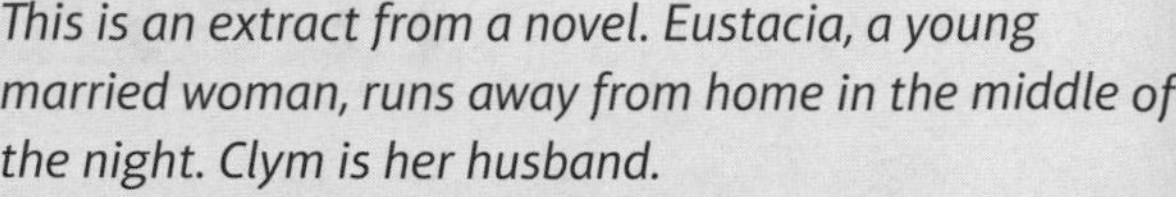

This is an extract from a novel. Eustacia, a young married woman, runs away from home in the middle of the night. Clym is her husband.

The Return of the Native: Thomas Hardy

He went on to the landing, and stood waiting nearly five minutes. Still she did not return. He went back for a light, and prepared to follow her; but first he looked into her bedroom. There, on the outside of the quilt, was the impression of her form[1], showing that the bed had not been opened; and, what was more significant, she had not taken her candlestick downstairs. He was now thoroughly alarmed; and hastily putting on his clothes he descended to the front door, which he himself had bolted and locked. It was now unfastened. There was no longer any doubt that Eustacia had left the house at this midnight hour; and whither could she have gone? To follow her was almost impossible. Had the dwelling stood in an ordinary road, two persons setting out, one in each direction, might have made sure of overtaking her; but it was a hopeless task to seek for anybody on a heath in the dark, the practicable directions for flight across it from any point being as numerous as the meridians[2] radiating from the pole[3]. Perplexed what to do, he looked into the parlour, and was vexed[4] to find that the letter still lay there untouched.

At half-past eleven, finding that the house was silent, Eustacia had lighted her candle, put on some warm outer wrappings, taken her bag in her hand, and, extinguishing the light again, descended the staircase. When she got into the outer air she found that it had begun to rain, and as she stood pausing at the door it increased, threatening to come on heavily. But having committed herself to this line of action there was no retreating for bad weather. Even the receipt of Clym's letter would not have stopped her now. The gloom of the night was funereal[5]; all nature seemed clothed in crape[6]. The spiky points of the fir trees behind the house rose into the sky like the turrets and pinnacles of an abbey. Nothing below the horizon was visible save a light which was still burning in the cottage of Susan Nunsuch.

Eustacia opened her umbrella and went out from the enclosure by the steps over the bank, after which she was beyond all danger of being perceived. Skirting the pool, she followed the path towards Rainbarrow, occasionally stumbling over twisted furze roots, tufts of rushes, or oozing lumps of fleshy fungi, which at this season lay scattered about the heath like the rotten liver and lungs of some colossal animal. The moon and stars were closed up by cloud and rain to the degree of extinction. It was a night which led the traveller's thoughts instinctively to dwell on nocturnal scenes of disaster in the chronicles of the world, on all that is terrible and dark in history and legend – the last plague of Egypt, the destruction of Sennacherib's host, the agony in Gethsemane.

Eustacia at length reached Rainbarrow, and stood still there to think. Never was harmony more perfect than that between the chaos of her mind and the chaos of the world without. A sudden recollection had flashed on her this moment – she had not money enough for undertaking a long journey. Amid the fluctuating sentiments of the day her unpractical mind had not dwelt on the necessity of being well-provided, and now that she thoroughly realized the conditions she sighed bitterly and ceased to stand erect, gradually crouching down under the umbrella as if she were drawn into the Barrow by a hand from beneath. Could it be that she was to remain a captive still? Money—she had never felt its value before. Even to efface[7] herself from the country means were required.

1: *form* – body
2: *meridians* – circles
3: *pole* – e.g. the North Pole
4: *vexed* – annoyed or worried
5: *funereal* – dark and depressing
6: *crape* – black silk
7: *efface* – erase, remove

Cut along the dotted lines and staple the texts together to make your own handy anthology. Make sure you keep it safe with your Workbook.

Text 2

This is an extract from a novel. Peter Malone, a curate, is on his way to Hollow's Mill to check on the inhabitants of the nearby cottage.

Shirley: Charlotte Brontë

The evening was pitch dark: star and moon were quenched in gray rain-clouds – gray they would have been by day; by night they looked sable[1]. Malone was not a man given to close observation of nature; her changes passed, for the most part, unnoticed by him. He could walk miles on the most varying April day and never see the beautiful dallying of earth and heaven – never mark[2] when a sunbeam kissed the hill-tops, making them smile clear in green light, or when a shower wept over them, hiding their crests[3] with the low-hanging, dishevelled tresses[4] of a cloud. He did not, therefore, care to contrast the sky as it now appeared – a muffled, streaming vault, all black, save where, towards the east, the furnaces of Stilbro' ironworks threw a tremulous lurid shimmer on the horizon – with the same sky on an unclouded frosty night. He did not trouble himself to ask where the constellations and the planets were gone, or to regret the "black-blue" serenity of the air-ocean which those white islets[5] stud, and which another ocean, of heavier and denser element, now rolled below and concealed. He just doggedly pursued his way, leaning a little forward as he walked, and wearing his hat on the back of his head, as his Irish manner was. "Tramp, tramp," he went along the causeway, where the road boasted the privilege of such an accommodation; "splash, splash," through the mire-filled cart ruts, where the flags[6] were exchanged for soft mud. He looked but for certain landmarks – the spire of Briarfield Church; farther on, the lights of Redhouse. This was an inn; and when he reached it, the glow of a fire through a half-curtained window, a vision of glasses on a round table, and of revellers on an oaken settle, had nearly drawn aside the curate[7] from his course. He thought longingly of a tumbler of whisky-and-water. In a strange place he would instantly have realized the dream; but the company assembled in that kitchen were Mr. Helstone's own parishioners; they all knew him. He sighed, and passed on.

The highroad was now to be quitted, as the remaining distance to Hollow's Mill might be considerably reduced by a short cut across fields. These fields were level and monotonous. Malone took a direct course through them, jumping hedge and wall. He passed but one building here, and that seemed large and hall-like, though irregular. You could see a high gable[8], then a long front, then a low gable, then a thick, lofty stack of chimneys. There were some trees behind it. It was dark; not a candle shone from any window. It was absolutely still; the rain running from the eaves[9], and the rather wild but very low whistle of the wind round the chimneys and through the boughs were the sole sounds in its neighbourhood.

This building passed, the fields, hitherto flat, declined in a rapid descent. Evidently a vale lay below, through which you could hear the water run. One light glimmered in the depth. For that beacon Malone steered.

He came to a little white house – you could see it was white even through this dense darkness – and knocked at the door. A fresh-faced servant opened it. By the candle she held was revealed a narrow passage, terminating in a narrow stair. Two doors covered with crimson baize[10], a strip of crimson carpet down the steps, contrasted with light-coloured walls and white floor, made the little interior look clean and fresh.

1: *sable* – black
2: *mark* – notice
3: *crests* – tops
4: *dishevelled tresses* – the low cloud is being compared to long, untidy locks of hair
5: *islets* – small islands (here, a reference to the stars and planets)
6: *flags* – paving slabs or stones
7: *curate* – a vicar's assistant
8: *gable* – part of a wall, near the roof
9: *eaves* – parts of a roof
10: *baize* – felt-like material

Cut along the dotted lines and staple the texts together to make your own handy anthology. Make sure you keep it safe with your Workbook.

Text 3

This is an extract from a short story. Here, the narrator breaks the news of his engagement to his uncle, in whose house he lives.

The Poor Relation's Story: Charles Dickens

My life at my uncle Chill's was of a spare dull kind, and my garret chamber was as dull, and bare, and cold, as an upper prison room in some stern northern fortress. But, having Christiana's love, I wanted nothing upon earth. I would not have changed my lot with any human being.

Avarice[1] was, unhappily, my uncle Chill's master-vice. Though he was rich, he pinched, and scraped, and clutched, and lived miserably. As Christiana had no fortune, I was for some time a little fearful of confessing our engagement to him; but, at length I wrote him a letter, saying how it all truly was. I put it into his hand one night, on going to bed.

As I came down-stairs next morning, shivering in the cold December air; colder in my uncle's unwarmed house than in the street, where the winter sun did sometimes shine, and which was at all events enlivened by cheerful faces and voices passing along; I carried a heavy heart towards the long, low breakfast-room in which my uncle sat. It was a large room with a small fire, and there was a great bay window in it which the rain had marked in the night as if with the tears of houseless people. It stared upon a raw yard, with a cracked stone pavement, and some rusted iron railings half uprooted, whence an ugly out-building that had once been a dissecting-room (in the time of the great surgeon who had mortgaged the house to my uncle), stared at it.

We rose so early always, that at that time of the year we breakfasted by candle-light. When I went into the room, my uncle was so contracted by the cold, and so huddled together in his chair behind the one dim candle, that I did not see him until I was close to the table.

As I held out my hand to him, he caught up his stick (being infirm, he always walked about the house with a stick), and made a blow at me, and said, "You fool!"

"Uncle," I returned, "I didn't expect you to be so angry as this." Nor had I expected it, though he was a hard and angry old man.

"You didn't expect!" said he; "when did you ever expect? When did you ever calculate, or look forward, you contemptible dog?"

"These are hard words, uncle!"

"Hard words? Feathers, to pelt such an idiot as you with," said he. "Here! Betsy Snap! Look at him!"

Betsy Snap was a withered, hard-favoured[2], yellow old woman – our only domestic – always employed, at this time of the morning, in rubbing my uncle's legs. As my uncle adjured her to look at me, he put his lean grip on the crown of her head, she kneeling beside him, and turned her face towards me. An involuntary thought connecting them both with the Dissecting Room, as it must often have been in the surgeon's time, passed across my mind in the midst of my anxiety.

"Look at the snivelling milksop!"[3] said my uncle. "Look at the baby! This is the gentleman who, people say, is nobody's enemy but his own. This is the gentleman who can't say no. This is the gentleman who was making such large profits in his business that he must needs take a partner, t'other day. This is the gentleman who is going to marry a wife without a penny, and who falls into the hands of Jezabels[4] who are speculating on my death!"

I knew, now, how great my uncle's rage was; for nothing short of his being almost beside himself would have induced him to utter that concluding word, which he held in such repugnance[5] that it was never spoken or hinted at before him on any account.

"On my death," he repeated, as if he were defying me by defying his own abhorrence[6] of the word. "On my death – death – Death! But I'll spoil the speculation. Eat your last under this roof, you feeble wretch, and may it choke you!"

1: *avarice* – extreme greed
2: *hard-favoured* – unattractive
3: *milksop* – pathetic man
4: *Jezabels* – shameless women
5: *repugnance* – intense disgust
6: *abhorrence* – disgust

Cut along the dotted lines and staple the texts together to make your own handy anthology. Make sure you keep it safe with your Workbook.

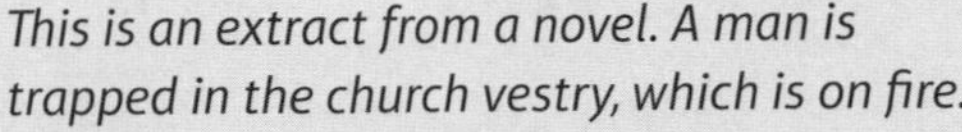

Text 4

This is an extract from a novel. A man is trapped in the church vestry, which is on fire.

The Woman in White: Wilkie Collins

I looked round at my two companions. The servant had risen to his feet – he had taken the lantern, and was holding it up vacantly at the door. Terror seemed to have struck him with downright idiocy – he waited at my heels, he followed me about when I moved like a dog. The clerk sat crouched up on one of the tombstones, shivering, and moaning to himself. The one moment in which I looked at them was enough to show me that they were both helpless.

Hardly knowing what I did, acting desperately on the first impulse that occurred to me, I seized the servant and pushed him against the vestry[1] wall. "Stoop!" I said, "and hold by the stones. I am going to climb over you to the roof – I am going to break the skylight, and give him some air!"

The man trembled from head to foot, but he held firm. I got on his back, with my cudgel[2] in my mouth, seized the parapet with both hands, and was instantly on the roof. In the frantic hurry and agitation of the moment, it never struck me that I might let out the flame instead of letting in the air. I struck at the skylight, and battered in the cracked, loosened glass at a blow. The fire leaped out like a wild beast from its lair. If the wind had not chanced, in the position I occupied, to set it away from me, my exertions might have ended then and there. I crouched on the roof as the smoke poured out above me with the flame. The gleams and flashes of the light showed me the servant's face staring up vacantly under the wall – the clerk risen to his feet on the tombstone, wringing his hands in despair – and the scanty population of the village, haggard men and terrified women, clustered beyond in the churchyard – all appearing and disappearing, in the red of the dreadful glare, in the black of the choking smoke. And the man beneath my feet! – the man, suffocating, burning, dying so near us all, so utterly beyond our reach!

The thought half maddened me. I lowered myself from the roof, by my hands, and dropped to the ground.

"The key of the church!" I shouted to the clerk. "We must try it that way – we may save him yet if we can burst open the inner door."

"No, no, no!" cried the old man. "No hope! the church key and the vestry key are on the same ring – both inside there! Oh, sir, he's past saving – he's dust and ashes by this time!"

"They'll see the fire from the town," said a voice from among the men behind me. "There's a ingine in the town. They'll save the church."

I called to that man – *he* had his wits about him – I called to him to come and speak to me. It would be a quarter of an hour at least before the town engine could reach us. The horror of remaining inactive all that time was more than I could face. In defiance of my own reason I persuaded myself that the doomed and lost wretch in the vestry might still be lying senseless on the floor, might not be dead yet. If we broke open the door, might we save him? I knew the strength of the heavy lock – I knew the thickness of the nailed oak – I knew the hopelessness of assailing[3] the one and the other by ordinary means. But surely there were beams still left in the dismantled cottages near the church? What if we got one, and used it as a battering-ram against the door?

1: *vestry* – a room in a church, used as an office and for changing into ceremonial clothes
2: *cudgel* – a short, thick stick used as a weapon
3: *assailing* – attacking

TEXTS

Cut along the dotted lines and staple the texts together to make your own handy anthology. Make sure you keep it safe with your Workbook.

Text 5

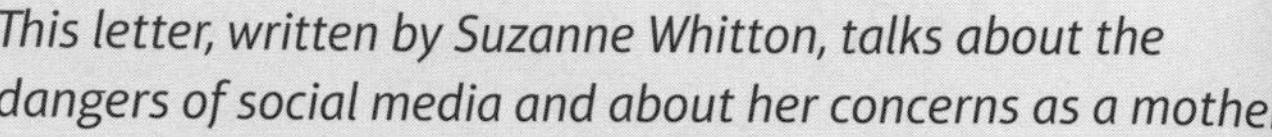
This letter, written by Suzanne Whitton, talks about the dangers of social media and about her concerns as a mother.

Dear daughter

Dear daughter,

I know you will think I'm daft, writing to you instead of talking, but something happens to children when they hit a certain age – mum suddenly becomes a dinosaur that is best put on mute!

You might think this barmy old dinosaur doesn't get it. I do. So please give my words a chance.

You're 15 now and maturing into an intelligent, independent young lady – and I am proud to call you my daughter. But like all young people today, you're susceptible to the pressures and pitfalls of the pacey technological age we live in. What am I on about? Social media.

Back in the dark ages, when I was a teenager, the only way I could get hold of my friends when I was back home after school was the telephone. A massive landline telephone, with a cable and everything. But I did contact them – like you, I wanted to share my thoughts and feelings.

But the social media of today is different. And it's not real life. You really need to understand this. It presents us with tiny snippets of someone's day that have been posed for, meticulously[1] selected, edited and that are sometimes even fabricated.

What saddens me most is seeing young girls, even younger than you, posing seductively in front of the camera, pouting into the lens and ageing at least 10 years in a single click. What are they saying to the world? What message are they sending out to boys… or even to men twice their age?

A dangerous one.

Dangerous because these are alluring images, but also because it's not real life.

Please don't look at these doctored images of other people's lives and assume yours is a much poorer version. It really isn't. You can't compare your reality to someone else's edited headline and that's all it is – an edited headline.

I am proud to call you my daughter. But no matter what age you are and however grown up you perceive yourself to be, I will always be your mum. My number one job in life is to guard your heart and that includes making you aware of life's pitfalls. For you, a world without social media would be a total disaster. For me, it would make my job as a parent so much easier.

Please think before you press 'send' on a provocative image. Think about who will see it and what it says about you. Think about your future self, 10 years from now, the one who will be finishing university and pitching[2] for those high-flying jobs, as I know you will be. What will potential employers say when they see your online history? I know this probably seems like a million years away to you, but it'll be here in a flash. Don't let a thoughtless click now affect your chances of success then.

I'm not asking you to stop using social media – we both know that would make me a hypocrite. I just want you to pause for a second before hitting 'send' and to keep that sensible head of yours screwed on tight.

This barmy old dinosaur wants the best for you in life. Always remember that.

Your ever-loving Mum x

1: *meticulously* – very carefully
2: *pitching* – applying

Cut along the dotted lines and staple the texts together to make your own handy anthology. Make sure you keep it safe with your Workbook.

Text 6

This is a newspaper article by Michele Hanson about the challenges of teaching teenagers.

OK, you try teaching 13-year-olds

Shocking news: a young trainee languages teacher on placement at Tarleton High in Lancashire "lost it" in class, barricaded the door with furniture, trapping the pupils, and threatened to kill them with something nasty that she had in her handbag. But why shocking? Imagine yourself in her place, "teaching" about 30 13- or 14-year-old creatures. Do you have one or two in your house? Are they polite, quiet and cooperative? Or are they breathtakingly insolent[1], noisy, crabby, offensive, skulking, smoking, drugging, and whingeing that they are not suitably entertained? What if you had 30? Wouldn't you like something in your handbag to shut the little toads up?

I'm trying not to sound bitter here, but I have taught; I have known supply-teaching hell; and I, too, have blown my top, even though it was 3.30pm and nearly over, because by then they were still climbing up walls (really), throwing scissors, dribbling glue and screaming all the while ... and when that happens, sometimes one just cannot keep one's cool a second longer.

And 13 is a particularly cruel age. In my first year's teaching, I crashed the car and sliced my forehead open on the sun-visor. Back at school, with my unsightly 27-stitch scar, I passed two 13-year-old girls. "She looks uglier than ever," said they, laughing merrily.

To be a teacher, one must be calm, sensible, tough, smartly dressed ALL THE TIME, and attractive. Otherwise, you are done for. Any degree of sensitivity can be a handicap. I blame the parents, partly. They often think teacher is a child-minding serf[2] and their huge babies are innocent and truthful. A big mistake.

Now think of that young teacher. "She had been trying to get them to be quiet," we learn. So she had probably been shouted at and humiliated for 40 minutes. This was her very last day of several horrible weeks of a placement. The end of her torment was a whisker away, but, driven barmy by pupils, she still blew it. Her career is now ruined. But the children were "petrified ... burst into tears" and were offered "support". The pathetic little wets[3]. She was pretending, you fools – dredging up a last desperate ploy[4] to shut the monsters up. If she had cried, they would have laughed out loud. Hopefully, she won't be sacked. If that's what she really, really wants.

Michele Hanson

The Guardian

1: *insolent* – rude and disrespectful
2: *serf* – slave
3: *wets* – feeble, pathetic people
4: *ploy* – cunning plan

Cut along the dotted lines and staple the texts together to make your own handy anthology. Make sure you keep it safe with your Workbook.

Text 7

John F. Kennedy was President of the United States from 1961 to 1963. He gave this speech at Rice University in 196 when the space race with the Soviet Union was at its heigh

We choose to go to the moon

No man can fully grasp how far and how fast we have come, but condense, if you will, the 50,000 years of man's recorded history into a time span of but a half-century. Stated in these terms, we know very little about the first 40 years, except at the end of them advanced man had learned to use the skins of animals to cover them. Then about 10 years ago, under this standard, man emerged from his caves to construct other kinds of shelter. Only five years ago man learned to write and use a cart with wheels. Christianity began less than two years ago. The printing press came this year, and then less than two months ago, during this whole 50-year span of human history, the steam engine provided a new source of power.

Newton explored the meaning of gravity. Last month electric lights and telephones and automobiles and airplanes became available. Only last week did we develop penicillin[1] and television and nuclear power, and now if America's new spacecraft succeeds in reaching Venus, we will have literally reached the stars before midnight tonight.

This is a breathtaking pace, and such a pace cannot help but create new ills as it dispels[2] old, new ignorance, new problems, new dangers. Surely the opening vistas of space promise high costs and hardships, as well as high reward. …

If this capsule history[3] of our progress teaches us anything, it is that man, in his quest for knowledge and progress, is determined and cannot be deterred. The exploration of space will go ahead, whether we join in it or not, and it is one of the great adventures of all time, and no nation which expects to be the leader of other nations can expect to stay behind in the race for space.

Those who came before us made certain that this country rode the first waves of the industrial revolutions, the first waves of modern invention, and the first wave of nuclear power, and this generation does not intend to founder in the backwash of the coming age of space. We mean to be a part of it – we mean to lead it. For the eyes of the world now look into space, to the moon and to the planets beyond, and we have vowed that we shall not see it governed by a hostile flag of conquest, but by a banner of freedom and peace. We have vowed that we shall not see space filled with weapons of mass destruction, but with instruments of knowledge and understanding. …

We set sail on this new sea because there is new knowledge to be gained, and new rights to be won, and they must be won and used for the progress of all people. For space science, like nuclear science and all technology, has no conscience of its own. Whether it will become a force for good or ill depends on man, and only if the United States occupies a position of pre-eminence can we help decide whether this new ocean will be a sea of peace or a new terrifying theater of war. I do not say that we should or will go unprotected against the hostile misuse of space any more than we go unprotected against the hostile use of land or sea, but I do say that space can be explored and mastered without feeding the fires of war, without repeating the mistakes that man has made in extending his writ[4] around this globe of ours.

There is no strife, no prejudice, no national conflict in outer space as yet. Its hazards are hostile to us all. Its conquest deserves the best of all mankind, and its opportunity for peaceful cooperation may never come again. But why, some say, the moon? Why choose this as our goal? And they may well ask why climb the highest mountain? Why, 35 years ago, fly the Atlantic? …

We choose to go to the moon. We choose to go to the moon in this decade and do the other things, not because they are easy, but because they are hard, because that goal will serve to organize and measure the best of our energies and skills, because that challenge is one that we are willing to accept, one we are unwilling to postpone, and one which we intend to win, and the others, too.

1: *penicillin* – an antibiotic medicine
2: *dispels* – gets rid of
3: *capsule history* – condensed or shortened history
4: *writ* – authority, power

Text 8

This text is from a newspaper article by John Arlidge about technology that is designed to control moods.

'Appy ever after'

"Try to relax," says Isy Goldwasser. It should be easy. I've had seven hours' sleep, coffee and eggs for breakfast. It's 10am but it's already 27ºC. I'm sitting in a picture-book-pretty converted 19th-century opera house that now serves as Goldwasser's office at the centre of Los Gatos, one of the most prosperous towns in Silicon Valley[1]. The trouble is, Goldwasser has just attached two electrodes to my head and is about to start pumping electricity straight into my brain.

In the home of moonshots[2] and "anything goes" optimism, the serial entrepreneur[3] Goldwasser and his business partner, the neuroscientist[4] Dr Jamie Tyler, are the most off-the-chart business brains you'll find. "We'll soon launch a consumer electronics product that you can use to shift your state of mind," Goldwasser assures me as he hands me the machine that controls how much electricity flows from the electrodes through my skull.

You mean hack my brain to make me feel what I want to feel, rather than what I actually do feel? I ask. "Yeah. We want to marry neuroscience and consumer electronics."

He hands me the controller. I select Calm mode. I turn the dial up and – *Holy silicon mad professors*! – it hurts. There's a sharp vibration that feels like the neurons[5] in my head are pogoing[6]. Not relaxing at all. I turn it down and wait. And then something remarkable happens. After a few minutes, I begin to feel waves gently flowing through my head. I don't notice at first but soon I begin to slump in my chair, my pupils dilate and my breathing slows. I really do begin to feel more relaxed. I have another go for 20 minutes and the same thing happens.

"See!" says Goldwasser, not at all calmly.

Next year Thync, Goldwasser and Tyler's company, will launch the consumer version of the product I'm testing. The two men won't go into detail because the design is still confidential. But the electrodes, which will come with a mini power pack, will be small enough to fit in the palm of your hand and be simple to attach to your head. They are likely to be controlled using a mobile phone app. You will use the app to select the mood you want to be in and determine how much current flows into your brain, using a simple slide bar. Two modes – moods – will be on offer first: calm and energy. More will follow. Thync is focusing on willpower, self-control, motivation, confidence and creativity.

Goldwasser believes harnessing willpower will have big implications in the treatment of obesity, alcoholism or gambling addiction…

Mankind has used mood-altering substances ever since we discovered alcohol, coffee and tobacco and later drugs, prescription or otherwise. Goldwasser and Tyler want to add that to the list of little helpers neuro-signalling algorithms[7], to give their brainwave technology its fancy name. Goldwasser, former president of the materials sciences company Symyx Technologies, and Tyler, a professor at Arizona State University, argue that "unlocking the power of the mind – regulating[8] biology with technology – is the biggest new frontier of this century and will be one of the greatest advances of our lifetime. We're kicking it off."

Goldwasser and Tyler may sound bonkers, but if their timing is anything to go by, they're the smartest guys in the lab. Wearable gizmos are the hottest new sector in the trillion-pound global technology sector. Apple launches its first smartwatch in the new year and will be followed by wearable kit from Microsoft and Google, which promises new versions of its web-enabled spectacles, Google Glass. Many of the new devices are designed to improve our health by monitoring our blood pressure and our stress levels, keeping tabs on how much exercise we take and helping us to feel refreshed in the morning by waking us up as we are coming out of a period of deep sleep. Goldwasser and Tyler are taking the idea one step further, giving us the power to change the way we feel, whenever we want.

"Tap into your self-control. Tap into your creativity. Tap into your energy. Tap into your calm. Think of us as your third cup of coffee in the morning or your glass of wine at night," Goldwasser smiles.

John Arlidge

The Sunday Times, 30 November 2014

1: *Silicon Valley* – an area in the United States, famous for its technology businesses
2: *moonshots* – ambitious projects
3: *serial entrepreneur* – someone who keeps setting up new businesses
4: *neuroscientist* – a scientist specialising in the nervous system and the brain
5: *neurons* – cells that transmit nerve signals
6: *pogoing* – jumping up and down
7: *neuro-signalling algorithms* – processes that signal nerve pathways
8: *regulating* – controlling

Cut along the dotted lines and staple the texts together to make your own handy anthology. Make sure you keep it safe with your Workbook.

Text 9

Clive James is an Australian-British writer, critic and broadcaster. Unreliable Memoirs *is the first volume of his autobiography, in which he describes his childhood in Australia.*

Unreliable Memoirs

Such catastrophes distressed my mother but she wrote them off as growing pains. Other exploits broke her heart. Once when she was out shopping I was riding my second-hand Malvern Star 26-inch frame bicycle around the house on a complicated circuit which led from the back yard along the driveway, once around a small fir tree that stood in the front yard, and back along the narrow side passage. Passing boys noticed what I was up to and came riding in. In a while there were a dozen or so of us circulating endlessly against the clock. Once again I could not leave well alone. I organised a spectacular finish in which the riders had to plunge into my mother's prize privet[1] hedge. The idea was for the bike's front wheel to lodge in the thick privet and the rider to fall dramatically into the bush and disappear. It became harder and harder to disappear as the privet became more and more reduced to ruins.

Giddy with success, I started doing the same thing to the hydrangeas. Finally I did it to the fir tree, ramming it with the bike and falling through it, thereby splitting its trunk. When my mother came wearily down the street with the shopping she must have thought the house had been strafed[2]. I was hiding under it – a sure sign of advanced guilt and fear, since it was dark under there and red-backs[3] were plentiful. She chased me up the peach tree and hit me around the ankles with a willow wand. It didn't hurt me as much as her tears did. Not for the only time, I heard her tell me that I was more than she could cope with. I suppose there was a possibility that I somehow felt compelled to go on reminding her of that fact.

Bombing my bed didn't make me very popular either. It was a trick I learned while recovering from mumps. Climbing on to the top of the wardrobe in my room, I would jump off and land on my bed, which seemed an immense distance below. Actually it was only a few feet, but the bed groaned satisfactorily. Eventually there were half a dozen of us climbing up and jumping off in rapid succession. It was a mistake to let Graham Truscott play. He had a double chin even at that age and a behind like a large bag of soil. But it took him so long to climb the wardrobe that it seemed unreasonable not to let him jump off it. The frame of the bed snapped off its supports with the noise of a firing squad and crashed to the floor with the roar of a cannon. I sent everyone home and tried to restore the bed to its right height by putting suitcases under it, but all that did was cave in the suitcases. Once again it was very dark under the house.

1: *privet* – a type of shrub
2: *strafed* – attacked by aircraft with machine guns
3: *red-backs* – highly poisonous spiders native to Australia

Cut along the dotted lines and staple the texts together to make your own handy anthology. Make sure you keep it safe with your Workbook.

Text 10

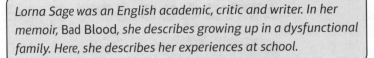

Lorna Sage was an English academic, critic and writer. In her memoir, Bad Blood, *she describes growing up in a dysfunctional family. Here, she describes her experiences at school.*

Bad Blood

Where were we? We'd only once had a geography lesson at Hanmer school, one sunny morning when Mr Palmer with a flourish draped a cracked and shiny blue-green-brown map over the blackboard next to his desk and sat surveying us, tapping his pointer gently in the palm of his left hand. Geography was a game. He'd call out a name – Manchester or Swansea or Carlisle – and one by one we had to walk up to the board and point at it. Any straying finger got a sharp rap from Mr Palmer's stick. Naturally most of us got it wrong, since we'd never seen a map of the British Isles before. The only way to win at this game was to approach very slowly and see if you could spot your town in time, but since most kids couldn't read very well (or at all) this didn't help a lot. I did all right with something beginning with B (Bolton or Blackburn or Birkenhead or Birmingham) but I cried anyway, I always did. Although we may not have found out much about geography that day, we were being taught a lesson, the usual one: to know our place. Hanmer wasn't on the map and Hanmer was where we were. Most of us, according to Mr Palmer, would be muck-shovellers[1]. Two or three of us, equally pawns in the game, would be allowed to get away with it – this time.

Hanmer school's best moments had been the times when no one pretended we were being taught, when fun was decreed with no forfeits[2] – like the warm-up session for the Christmas party when Mr Palmer, a beaming ogre, led us in carols and nonsense songs, ending with an ear-splitting, hysterical chorus, 'Ooooh, the Okey Cokey! That's what it's *all abOUT*!' Or the summer PT lesson when we ran up a bench propped against the churchyard wall, round some gravestones, through the bindweed and nettles – this corner beetling over the schoolyard hadn't been used for a century – and down another bench into the playground again. Or the day of deep frost one winter when the big boys were sent out with buckets of water to make a slide on the field below the bike shed and we all took turns, marvelling at the long green grass trapped flowing in the ice under our feet like seaweed.

My brother had already started on his school career and would in time be promoted to carrying coke[3] for the cast-iron classroom stoves – perhaps in fulfilment of Mr Palmer's theory of hereditary roles, for Clive was in everyone's eyes much more a Stockton. His time at Hanmer school would leave him with a legacy of fiery temper tantrums. In my case its frustrations, mystifications and menace made me chronically shifty. You learned at Hanmer school to keep the world of grown-up authority out of focus, to look askance[4], to stare stubbornly at an invisible point in the air between yourself and them. You learned to seem dull and stupid. I was no exception. Mr Palmer may have massaged my results to match my vicarage IQ, but I was far too scared of him to feel any complicity. And – although I didn't know it at the time – Miss Myra and Miss Daisy regarded me with special distaste, as the granddaughter of the old devil who'd corrupted their niece Marj. My being bookish hadn't brought me any closer to my teachers than any of the other children.

1: *muck-shovellers* – farm workers
2: *forfeits* – penalties
3: *coke* – a solid fuel made from coal
4: *askance* – with suspicion

Images for questions on page 48

Image A

Image B

Images for questions on page 61

Image C

Image D

Timed test

Edexcel publishes official Sample Assessment Material on its website. This timed test has been written to help you practise what you have learned and may not be representative of a real exam paper.

In the exam, you will be given space to write in. Here, **you will need to use your own paper for your answers**.

GCSE English Language

Paper 1: Fiction and Imaginative Writing

Time: 1 hour 45 minutes

Instructions

- Answer **all** questions in Section A and **ONE** in Section B.
- You should spend about 1 hour on Section A.
- You should spend about 45 minutes on Section B.

Advice

- Read each question carefully before you start to answer it.
- Check your answers if you have time at the end.

SECTION A – Reading text

Read the text below and answer Questions 1–4 on the question paper.

This is an extract from a novel. A family discuss a mysterious young woman who has come to live in a nearby hall.

***The Tenant of Wildfell Hall*: Anne Brontë**

'Well,' resumed Rose; 'I was going to tell you an important piece of news I heard there – I have been bursting with it ever since. You know it was reported a month ago, that somebody was going to take Wildfell Hall – and – what do you think? It has actually been inhabited above a week! – and we never knew!'

'Impossible!' cried my mother.

'Preposterous!!!' shrieked Fergus.

'It has indeed! – and by a single lady!'

'Good gracious, my dear! The place is in ruins!'

'She has had two or three rooms made habitable; and there she lives, all alone – except an old woman for a servant!'

'Oh, dear! that spoils it – I'd hoped she was a witch,' observed Fergus, while carving his inch-thick slice of bread and butter.

'Nonsense, Fergus! But isn't it strange, mamma?'

'Strange! I can hardly believe it.'

'But you may believe it; for Jane Wilson has seen her. She went with her mother, who, of course, when she heard of a stranger being in the neighbourhood, would be on pins and needles till she had seen her and got all she could out of her. She is called Mrs. Graham, and she is in mourning – not widow's weeds[1], but slightish mourning – and she is quite young, they say, – not above five or six and twenty, – but so reserved! They tried all they could to find out who she was and where she came from, and, all about her, but neither Mrs. Wilson, with her pertinacious[2] and impertinent home-thrusts[3], nor Miss Wilson, with her skilful manoeuvring, could manage to elicit a single satisfactory answer, or even a casual remark, or chance expression calculated to allay[4] their curiosity, or throw the faintest ray of light upon her history, circumstances, or connections. Moreover, she was barely civil to them, and evidently better pleased to say 'good-by,' than 'how do you do.' But Eliza Millward says her father intends to call upon her soon, to offer some pastoral advice, which he fears she needs, as, though she is known to have entered the neighbourhood early last week, she did not make her appearance at church on Sunday; and she – Eliza, that is – will beg to accompany him, and is sure she can succeed in wheedling something out of her – you know, Gilbert, she can do anything. And we should call some time, mamma; it's only proper, you know.'

'Of course, my dear. Poor thing! How lonely she must feel!'

'And pray, be quick about it; and mind you bring me word how much sugar she puts in her tea, and what sort of caps and aprons she wears, and all about it; for I don't know how I can live till I know,' said Fergus, very gravely.

But if he intended the speech to be hailed as a master-stroke of wit, he signally failed, for nobody laughed. However, he was not much disconcerted at that; for when he had taken a mouthful of bread and butter and was about to swallow a gulp of tea, the humour of the thing burst upon him with such irresistible force, that he was obliged to jump up from the table, and rush snorting and choking from the room; and a minute after, was heard screaming in fearful agony in the garden.

As for me, I was hungry, and contented myself with silently demolishing the tea, ham, and toast, while my mother and sister went on talking, and continued to discuss the apparent or non-apparent circumstances, and probable or improbable history of the mysterious lady; but I must confess that, after my brother's misadventure, I once or twice raised the cup to my lips, and put it down again without daring to taste the contents, lest I should injure my dignity by a similar explosion.

1: *widow's weeds* – black clothes worn by a widow in mourning
2: *pertinacious* – stubborn
3: *home-thrusts* – personal attacks
4: *allay* – reduce, calm

SECTION A – Reading

Read the text provided above and answer ALL questions.
You should spend about 1 hour on this section.

1 From lines 1–9, identify the phrase which explains why the family is surprised that Wildfell Hall has a tenant. **(1 mark)**

2 From lines 14–25, give **two** reasons why Jane Wilson might have felt unwelcome when she visited the new neighbour Mrs Graham.
You may use your own words or quotation from the text. **(2 marks)**

3 In lines 25–35, how does the writer use language and structure to show the different reactions of the family towards the new neighbour?
Support your views with reference to the text. **(6 marks)**

4 In this extract, the writer attempts to show the excitement created by a new neighbour.
Evaluate how successfully this is achieved.
Support your views with detailed reference to the text. **(15 marks)**

SECTION B – Imaginative Writing

Answer ONE question. You should spend about 45 minutes on this section.

EITHER

***5** Write about a time when you, or someone you know, met somebody new.
Your response could be real or imagined.

** Your response will be marked for the accurate and appropriate use of vocabulary, spelling, punctuation and grammar.* **(40 marks)**

OR

***6** Look at the images provided.
Write about a mysterious place.
Your response could be real or imagined. You may wish to base your response on one of the images.

** Your response will be marked for the accurate and appropriate use of vocabulary, spelling, punctuation and grammar.* **(40 marks)**

Timed test

Edexcel publishes official Sample Assessment Material on its website. This timed test has been written to help you practise what you have learned and may not be representative of a real exam paper.

In the exam, you will be given space to write in. Here, **you will need to use your own paper for your answers.**

GCSE English Language

Paper 2: Non-fiction and Transactional Writing

Time: 2 hours

Instructions

- Answer **all** questions in Section A and **ONE** in Section B.
- You should spend about 1 hour and 15 minutes on Section A.
- You should spend about 45 minutes on Section B.

Advice

- Read each question carefully before you start to answer it.
- Check your answers if you have time at the end.

SECTION A – Reading texts

Read the text below and answer Questions 1–3 on the question paper.

Text 1

Peter Snow is an English writer and journalist. His book, Oxford Observed: Town and Gown, *describes the city of Oxford in the 1990s. In this extract, Snow explains how Oxford is a city that has very different aspects.*

Each year up to half a million visitors come to Oxford, making it the third most popular venue in Britain after London and York. Most pause only a few hours before fast-forwarding on to the next stop on the tourist itinerary. All the same, directly and indirectly, they leave behind a tidy pile of money – over £300 million a year according to one estimate. But in return Oxford has traditionally done little for them. 'Welcoming while not encouraging,' was one local councillor's exquisitely phrased formulation of policy. Underhotelled, without clear signposted routes and marshalling areas[1] and lacking until recently a proper tourist centre, the city has a poor record in regulating the human tide that wash its streets each summer.

Just what impressions of Oxford do the visitors carry away with them? Various versions are on offer. There are guided walking tours of varying reliability (the official ones are good, the others often walking mines of misinformation, overheard snippets of which are prized by the more knowledgeable natives.) The Madame Tussaud's-like tableaux[2] of *The Oxford Story*[3] present a mostly Gown[4] version, a steady progress of onward and upward, through scenes of violence and squalor to the academic excellence of today and with Town[5] rarely getting a look in. Other visitors get a more open-topped experience from the tourist buses that trundle round the city. Many visitors, though simply jam the streets, gazing blankly at the facades of colleges or trailing through Cornmarket's chain of eateries and retail outlets.

Probably they come expecting in the ancient cradle of colleges and quadrangles[6] some sort of historic time capsule or Athenian city state of the mind complete with gowned and learned figures gravely discoursing in the cloisters[7]. Certainly the spires and cloisters exist but they are interspersed – submerged even – *among all the other bits.* Those who go on bus tours must have at times the dislocating sense, as the buses traverse the cluttered terrace-land of East Oxford, of being allowed to see around the *back of the set*.

Even a walk around the centre can be a bewildering, not to say distressing, experience. Above soar the stones of the spires but, lower down, reality jump-cuts before your eyes: four square Saxon church; medieval college; postmodern office block; timbers and gables; pompous civic wedding cake of a public building. There are bits of Bath-style restoration, courts and closes teetering on the brink of tweeness, and there are shopping malls – the glitzy, blue hooped vulgarity of the Clarendon Centre, and, then, the Westgate, barracks-like without, within a soft bubble bath of illuminated spheres, like a mad dream of a pawnbroker, with, to top it all off, an oriental pagoda plonked surreally in front.

Oxford is a place that seems to choke on its own rich contrasts, a jumble of impression fragments, on which competing visions of the city can be projected and superimposed. There is medieval Oxford, county market town Oxford, university Oxford, modern city centre Oxford, industrial Oxford, suburban residential Oxford…None of the versions seem entirely to fit the face beneath. Indeed at times fiction overrides reality altogether: soon we shall have Oxford as Inspector Morse-land, a set of tourist trails as originally trodden by the super-sleuth, tripping the connections of a recollected episode on TV.

Somehow the city's new Gloucester Green development sums up the whole chaos of contrasts. Local opinion about it varies widely – from vulgar monstrosity to wittily exuberant extravaganza – but to me it is the perfect symbol of the modern city, a postmodern barock n'roll, a restless ransacking of the wardrobe of the past, emitting its clash of scales and styles, with just the right Oxford hints of illusion and unreality.

1: *marshalling areas* – assembly points, places to gather
2: *Madame Tussaud's-like tableaux* – famous waxwork displays of famous people
3: *The Oxford Story* – a local museum
4: *Gown* – the part of Oxford that is linked to the university
5: *Town* – the part of Oxford that is not involved with the university
6: *quadrangles* – open courtyard areas in a college
7: *cloisters* – covered walkways in a college
(Extract from *Oxford Observed: Town and Gown*, Peter Snow, John Murray, 1991)

Read the text below and answer Questions 4–7 on the question paper.

Text 2

This text is from a newspaper article by Sophie Scott about tourism in Oxfordshire.

Turnaround in tourism as visitor numbers shoot up

TOURISM across Oxfordshire has seen a sharp rise this summer, with the good weather and the Olympics legacy getting the credit. A total of 195,301 people used the county's visitor centres in the past four months compared to 174,785 this time last year, an increase of 12 per cent. The west of the county saw the highest rise, with 27 per cent more people using visitor centres in West Oxfordshire during April and July in 2013.

Richard Langridge, West Oxfordshire District Council cabinet member responsible for tourism, said: "I think it's two things; clearly our superb attractions here but also the Olympic and Paralympic legacy from last year's Games.

"The district council does do marketing overseas, especially the US market, and people have definitely been impacted by the Olympic factor.

"They are coming to London then into West Oxfordshire to go to Cotswold Wildlife Park, Burford and Blenheim Palace, among others."

Cotswold Wildlife Park owner Reggie Heyworth said this had been its best summer for ten years.

He said: "The great weather and the fact people are staying in England for holidays has had a great impact for us."

There were 17,523 visitors between the information centres in Welch Way, Witney, and High Street, Burford, 3,689 more than last year.

Oxford has also seen a boost this summer, thanks to soaring temperatures that reached 30°C during July. The visitor centre in Broad Street had 152,389 visitors between April and July, 12 per cent up on the previous year's 135,395.

Max Mason, owner of The Big Bang restaurant, went as far as importing 23 tonnes of sand to create a beach at the Oxford Castle to attract more punters. He said: "I really do think that last year's Olympics are really having an effect this summer.

"It has been a really good summer this year for tourists and I think Oxford is managing to sell itself a lot better."

Banbury Visitor Centre, in Spiceball Park Road, saw the smallest rise. It had 25,943 enquiries for the same period this year, only 400 up from last year.

While South Oxfordshire and Vale of White Horse District Councils do not run any tourist info centres, joint promotional website southernoxfordshire.com had 49,664 page views last month, 140 per cent more than 2012.

The councils' economic development manager Suzanne Malcolm said publicity has boosted traffic to its websites.

She said: "We have seen a particularly strong growth in Visit Midsomer[1]."

VISITORS ON THE RISE

- West Oxfordshire visitor centres – 17,523 compared to 13,834 during the same time in 2012 – 27 per cent rise
- Oxford visitor centre – 152,389 people compared to 135,395 during the same time in 2012 – 12 per cent rise
- Banbury visitor centre – 25,943 people compared to 25,556 during the same time in 2012 – 1.5 per cent rise

1: *Midsomer* – a reference to the popular television detective drama, *Midsomer Murders*, some of which is filmed in Oxfordshire

SECTION A – Reading

Read Text 1. Then answer Questions 1–3.
You should spend about 1 hour 15 minutes on the WHOLE of Section A (Questions 1–7).

1 In lines 26–33, identify **two** reasons why a trip to Oxford might be distressing for visitors. **(2 marks)**

2 Give **one** example from lines 13–19 of how the writer uses language to create an impression of Oxford.
Support your example with a detailed text reference. **(2 marks)**

3 Analyse how the writer uses language and structure to interest and engage readers.
Support your views with detailed reference to the text. **(15 marks)**

Read Text 2. Then answer Questions 4–6.

4 Which area of Oxfordshire saw the biggest rise in people going to the visitor centres? **(1 mark)**

5 Give **one** example from lines 6–10 of how the writer uses language to show that Oxfordshire has been successful in making people want to visit the area. **(1 mark)**

6 In her newspaper article, Sophie Scott attempts to engage the reader by using different details to explain the current popularity of Oxford as a visitor destination.
Evaluate how successfully this is achieved.
Support your views with detailed reference to the text. **(15 marks)**

Question 7 is about Text 1 and Text 2. Answer both parts of the question. Refer to both texts in your answers.

7 (a) The two texts give different views of Oxford as a city for visitors.
What similarities do both texts share about tourists in the city and about Oxford's success in attracting visitors?
Use evidence from both texts to support your answer. **(6 marks)**

(b) Compare how the writers of Text 1 and Text 2 present their ideas and perspectives about Oxford as a city.
Support your ideas with detailed reference to the texts. **(14 marks)**

SECTION B – Transactional Writing

Answer ONE question. You should spend about 45 minutes on this section.

EITHER

***8** Write a letter to your local council applying for a job as a junior tourist guide.
In your letter you could:

- state why you are interested in the position
- explain why you think you would make a good tourist guide, e.g. good knowledge of your local area, relationship-building skills, work experience
- describe the attractions and facilities that you think should be included in your guided tours, and explain why they would attract visitors

as well as any other ideas you might have.

** Your response will be marked for the accurate and appropriate use of vocabulary, spelling, punctuation and grammar.* **(40 marks)**

OR

***9** Write a review for your school newspaper of a place you have visited on holiday.
You could write about:

- what the place has to offer, e.g. history, culture, food
- who might want to visit the place, and why they might want to visit
- your opinions about the place and whether you would recommend it to others

as well as any other ideas you might have.

** Your response will be marked for the accurate and appropriate use of vocabulary, spelling, punctuation and grammar.* **(40 marks)**

Answers

SECTION A: READING

1. Planning your exam time

1 Paper 1: 10 minutes; Paper 2: 15 minutes
2 About 2 minutes (Note: You could choose to spend less than 2 minutes on your answer to save time for checking your work.)
3 Lines 8–15
4 About 15 minutes (Note: You could choose to spend 10–12 minutes on your answer to save time for checking your work.)
5 Two (both) texts
6 All options should be circled.

2. Reading texts explained

1 (a) Answer provided on page 2.
(b) For example: The use of 'gleams and flashes' and 'terrified women' creates a tense atmosphere of suspense.
2 (a) The only way to win at this game was to approach very slowly and <u>see if you could spot your town in time</u>, but since <u>most kids couldn't read very well (or at all)</u> this didn't help a lot. I did all right with something beginning with B (Bolton or Blackburn or Birkenhead or Birmingham) <u>but I cried anyway, I always did.</u> Although we may not have found out much about geography that day, we were being taught a lesson, the usual one: <u>to know our place</u>. Hanmer wasn't on the map and Hanmer was where we were. Most of us, according to Mr Palmer, <u>would be muck-shovellers.</u>
(b) Answers should use the evidence identified in Question 2 (a) to make the key point that the writer feels she was poorly treated at school as the teachers bullied the children and made them feel inadequate.

3. Reading questions explained 1

1 (a) Answer provided on page 3.
(b) Paper 1, Question 2: AO1(a)
(c) Paper 2, Question 2: AO2
(d) Paper 2, Question 4: AO1(a)
(e) Paper 2, Question 7 (a): AO1(b)

4. Reading questions explained 2

1 (a) Paper 1, Question 4: Answer provided on page 4.
(b) Paper 2, Question 6: AO4
(c) Paper 2, Question 7 (b): AO3
2 The following questions on page 3 should be ticked: Paper 1, Question 1; Paper 1, Question 2; Paper 2, Question 2.
3 You should use all of the extract or extracts.

5. Reading the questions

1 (a) Answer provided on page 5.
(b) 'give'
2 Paper 1, Question 3: 1 text; lines 7–12; 'language and structure', 'change in the weather'; about 12 minutes.
Paper 2, Question 6: 1 text; whole extract; 'harsh education', 'gain sympathy', 'evaluate'; about 15 minutes.
Paper 2, Question 7 (a): 2 (both) texts; all of each text; 'mothers worry', 'children taking risks', 'similarities'; about 6 minutes.
(Note: The calculation for the length of time to spend on each answer is based on about 2 minutes per mark for Paper 1 and about 1 minute per mark for Paper 2. You could choose to spend less time per mark to save time for checking your work.)

6. Skimming for the main idea or theme

1 (a) Answer provided on page 6.
(b) For example: The opening sentence suggests that the main idea will be the difficulties of teaching, although it also suggests **that the article will be about why teachers find it difficult to control their anger**.
2 For example: The end of the article suggests that whilst it is the students who get support, it is the teachers who suffer the most.
3 For example: The ideas expressed at the end of the article differ from those at the beginning. The beginning of the article suggests teachers are aggressive while the end suggests that their careers can be ruined by children's poor behaviour.
4 For example: The main idea in the article is that poor behaviour in schools can make life really difficult for teachers.

7. Annotating the texts

1 A, B, C and D
2 E – because annotated detail E falls outside the lines of the extract given in the question.
3 Answers should include four or five annotations. For example, the following would all create sympathy for the narrator:
- 'garret chamber', 'upper prison room' and 'fortress' – suggest narrator is trapped in very harsh conditions
- 'pinched, and scraped, and clutched' and 'lived miserably' – suggest narrator's uncle was difficult to live with
- 'we breakfasted by candle-light' – emphasises the hard life enforced by the narrator's uncle
- 'made a blow at me' and '"You fool"' – shows how harshly Uncle Chill treats the narrator
- '"contemptible dog"', '"snivelling milksop"' and '"baby"' – uncle insults narrator in each of his speeches, which shows the level of criticism the narrator receives.

8. Putting it into practice

1 (a) and (b) Answers should include four or five annotated words or phrases. For example:
- 'beyond all danger of being perceived' – foreshadows danger, ironic as nobody will be able to help her if she is in real danger
- 'stumbling' – verb shows she is unsteady on her feet and cannot see the ground clearly
- 'twisted furze roots' – adjective 'twisted' suggests the roots might trap her
- 'oozing lumps of fleshy fungi' – creates an image of disease and decay
- 'like the rotten liver and lungs of some colossal animal' – simile suggests death and decay
- 'extinction' – suggests the light has gone forever, foreshadows danger to come.

2 For example:
The writer suggests Eustacia is running towards danger by creating images of decay and death around her.

Nature is described in terms of disease and decay; for example, the fungi is 'oozing lumps' and the heath is 'like the rotten liver and lungs of some colossal animal'. This simile suggests Eustacia's surroundings are actually dying and the word 'extinction' foreshadows the danger to come as it suggests that the light has gone forever, as in death.
Eustacia is also said to be 'beyond all danger of being perceived', which ironically foreshadows the danger she will be in as nobody will be able to help her. The lack of light is a danger for Eustacia, too, as she is unable to see the ground clearly. She is therefore unsteady on her feet, and is 'stumbling' over 'twisted furze roots'. Here, the adjective 'twisted' reinforces the sense of danger, as it suggests the roots could actually trap her as she passes.

9. Putting it into practice

1 (a) and (b) Answers should include four or five annotated words or phrases. Examples from the first paragraph could include:
- 'Such catastrophes distressed my mother' and 'Other exploits' – his adventures were obviously a big part of his childhood, which suggests his experiences were quite wild and extreme
- how James gives full details of his 'complicated circuit' to show how much effort he put into his boyhood exploits
- 'against the clock' – suggests his exploits were competitive
- 'spectacular finish' and 'plunge' – makes his exploits sound very exciting
- 'fall dramatically' and 'disappear' – emphasise the excitement
- 'reduced to ruins' – entertains the reader by creating a comical image.

2 For example:
The phrases 'Such catastrophes' and 'Other exploits' in the opening sentences suggest that boyish adventures were a large and important part of James's childhood and that they were often quite wild. James attempts to entertain the reader by describing these adventures in great detail; for example, the 'complicated circuit' in the 'front yard' becomes a short story in the first paragraph.
Furthermore, his exploits are described as popular and competitive as they are 'against the clock'. They are exciting as they end with a 'spectacular finish' and a 'plunge' into a prize privet hedge. Readers will be entertained by the comedy here, as well as by the comical final image of the privet hedge 'reduced to ruins'.

10. Explicit information and ideas

1 Four
2 For example: Writing in full sentences, or copying long phrases, will waste time in the exam. It is only necessary to use the shortest possible quotation when giving explicit information.
3 'having Christiana's love'
4 Paper 2, Question 1 – any **two** of: 'calm, sensible, tough, smartly dressed, attractive'
Paper 2, Question 4 – Tarleton High

11. Implicit ideas

1 Life was dull. – Answer provided on page 11.
His room is cold. – Explicit
He feels trapped. – Implicit
His uncle is mean. – Implicit
He is scared of his uncle. – Answer provided on page 11.
2 Answers should include four ideas; for example:
(a) the servant holds the lantern but does not know why or what to do with it
(b) the servant cannot act for himself
(c) the servant follows the narrator about
(d) the servant copies the actions of the narrator.

12. Inference

1 Annotations could include:
- 'sudden recollection'
- 'flashed on her this moment'
- 'she had not money enough'
- 'unpractical mind'
- 'now that she thoroughly realized the conditions'.

2 (a) The extract suggests that Eustacia **has been too emotional to plan her journey properly; the phrase 'fluctuating sentiments' suggests that she has been preoccupied with her feelings.**
(b) **The phrase 'ceased to stand erect' creates the idea of a frightened animal and suggests that Eustacia is vulnerable.**
3 For example:
The narrator is presented as capable of making decisions quickly and instinctively under pressure, as he acts 'desperately' on his 'first impulse' rather than stopping to think. The words 'seized' and 'pushed' suggest **that he is able to take charge and is keen to act rather than discuss options. This is also shown by the way he issues clear instructions to the servant in spite of the 'frantic hurry and agitation of the moment'. The narrator's bravery and physical fitness are shown in the description of how he 'instantly' climbs onto the roof with 'my cudgel in my mouth'.**

13. Interpreting information and ideas

(a) 'susceptible to' – Answer provided on page 13.
(b) 'pitfalls' – Answer provided on page 13.
(c) 'pacey' – fast-moving.
(d) 'the dark ages' – years ago, which will seem like a very long time ago indeed to the teenage recipient of the letter.
(e) 'provocative' – intended to be seductive.

2 (a) At the top, in the attic
(b) The narrator compares his room to an 'upper prison room', which tells us that it is near the top of the house. This, and the description of the room, suggest that his 'garret chamber' is an attic.
3 (a) The noun 'domestic' suggests that Betsy Snap is a servant, as we are told that she is 'always employed'.
(b) The verb 'adjured' is followed by a description of how the narrator's uncle turns Betsy's head with his hand. This suggests that Betsy has little choice and is being commanded to look at the narrator.

14. Using evidence

1 The writer obviously feels very strongly about space travel as he wants America to 'lead' the race to space. He feels it is a global issue as the 'eyes of the world' are on it, and his use of the word 'vowed' suggests he **will stick to his promise to do everything in his power to make sure it does not become an area of conflict. These strong feelings about the space race being a peaceful mission are emphasised by the use of contrasts. Firstly, the writer contrasts the idea of a 'hostile flag' with the more positive image of a 'banner of freedom'. He then**

goes on to contrast 'weapons of mass destruction' with 'instruments of knowledge and understanding', which suggests that the writer feels strongly about space travel being used to advance mankind.

2 The writer feels that it is up to man to determine whether **space travel advances mankind or causes further global conflict. He feels that the US is the country to lead the exploration of space and that, while the country should not enter the race completely unprepared for conflict, they should enable space to be explored without creating opportunities for disputes with other countries.**

3 Points (a), (c) and (d).

15. Point – Evidence – Explain

1 Evidence B

2 Evidence B is the most effective because it is an example of a list of adjectives and therefore links directly to the point made.

3 Evidence: For example, she uses the words **'barricaded', 'trapping' and 'threatened'.**
Explanation B

4 For example: Explanation B is more effective because it is fully developed and more specific, suggesting that the teacher treated the children like prisoners. The word 'also' signals additional details, which explore the teacher's actions further.

16. Putting it into practice

Paper 1, Question 1 – 'not a man given to close observation of nature'.

Paper 1, Question 2 – for example, two of:

- the sky is 'all black'
- the sky is so dark you cannot see the planets
- there is a '"black-blue" serenity'
- dense clouds are rolling in.

Paper 1, Question 3 – answers could include these key points:

- 'but one building' – the narrator is alone
- 'hall-like, though irregular' – makes the building sound slightly sinister
- the building is described in detail – 'low gable, then a thick, lofty stack of chimneys' – which suggests it is important and powerful
- 'not a candle shone from any window' – the building is deserted, which suggests danger
- 'absolutely still' – sinister and eerie
- the only sounds are the weather – 'rain running from the eaves'
- the personification of the wind in 'wild but very low whistle' makes it sound threatening
- 'sole sounds in its neighbourhood' – the house is personified, which intensifies the suggestion of danger.

17. Putting it into practice

Paper 2, Question 3 – answers could include these key points:

- use of fact: 'a young trainee languages teacher on placement at Tarleton High', '27-stitch scar'
- use of opinion: '13 is a particularly cruel age', 'supply-teaching hell'
- use of expert evidence: 'I have taught', 'I passed two 13-year-old girls'
- rhetorical questions to persuade: 'Wouldn't you like something in your handbag ...?'
- use of verbs with connotations of violence to emphasise what teachers are driven to: 'barricaded', 'trapping', 'threatened'
- colloquial language to create sarcasm – '"lost it"', 'blown my top', 'blew it'
- language to present the students as weak and to minimise the teacher's reaction – 'little toads', 'huge babies', 'pathetic little wets'
- use of lists to reinforce points – the character of the students ('insolent, noisy, crabby, offensive ...') and what a teacher needs to be to succeed ('calm, sensible, tough, smartly dressed ...').

18. Word classes

1 Examples could include:
- noun – 'furniture', 'handbag'
- verb – answer provided on page 18
- adverb – answer provided on page 18
- adjective – 'insolent', 'noisy'.

2 For example: The lists of adjectives build up contrasting pictures in the reader's mind of what teenagers are like. For instance, 'polite, quiet and co-operative' creates a positive image, while 'insolent, noisy, crabby ...' creates a negative image. This will make the reader question their own view of teenagers.

3 For example:
(a) Adjective: 'muffled' suggests that the black sky is blocking out sound, creating a quiet atmosphere, and also that it feels a little suffocating.
(b) Adjective: 'streaming' suggests that the black of the sky is flowing everywhere and quickly covering the whole horizon.
(c) Verb: the action verb 'threw' makes the sky seem alive and almost threatening.
(d) Verb: 'rolled' suggests the momentum of the heavy cloud filling the sky and gives the impression of something unstoppable and destructive.

19. Connotations

1 (a) waves – something that cannot be stopped
backwash – waste water going backwards
banner – symbol of celebration; sign of protest
instruments – measuring devices; professional tools
(b) For example: The word 'waves' suggests that mankind's progress cannot be halted and the word 'backwash' suggests that those who do not keep up with modern discoveries risk being left behind like waste water. The word 'banner' shows that the writer feels enthusiastic about the space race as it suggests a celebration, while the use of the term 'instruments' suggests that space exploration is a scientific experiment that should be approached in a professional manner.

2 For example:
(a) The adjective 'fresh-faced' used to describe the servant has connotations of something young and new, which suggests that she may be inexperienced.
(b) The repeated adjective 'crimson' has connotations of both blood and danger, suggesting that the 'little white house' may not be as innocent as it first appears.

20. Figurative language

1 For example:
The writer uses the simile 'like the turrets and pinnacles of an abbey', which has connotations of **both a castle and a church, buildings which are grand, solemn and imposing.**
This suggests to the reader **that Eustacia's journey is very important, but also, now that she has left her home,**

that she is at the mercy of nature, which now rules over her surroundings.

2 For example: The writer uses the simile 'like a wild beast' to suggest that the fire is a force of nature, with the power of a wild animal. This suggests to the reader that the fire is out of control and will not easily be tamed by man.

3 For example: The writer personifies the sun in the phrases 'a sunbeam kissed the hill-tops' and 'making them smile'. As a kiss symbolises affection and a smile suggests happiness, this personification emphasises the peaceful harmony of the sky when the sun is shining.

21. Creation of character

1 The writer uses dialogue to show that the narrator is brave and impulsive. **For example, he 'shouted to the clerk' and uses the imperative 'must', which suggests that he is taking charge. He also says 'we may save him yet', which shows that he is determined to try anything. He is brave as he is willing to 'burst open the inner door' even though the others see his efforts as hopeless. For instance, the old man cries '"No, no, no!"' and another man seems to suggest that they should wait for the fire engines.**

2 Answers could include these key points:
- 'he caught up his stick' and 'made a blow at me' suggest uncle Chill is unfriendly and aggressive, and perhaps that uncle Chill is not as disabled as the stick suggests
- '"You fool!"' and '"you contemptible dog"' suggest Chill is rude and unkind
- '"when did you ever expect?"' shows Chill has a low opinion of the narrator, and suggests the narrator may be a man with little ambition or drive.

3 Answers could include the following key points.
Dialogue – Chill commands Betsy, which suggests she is under his control:
- '"Here! Betsy Snap! Look at him!"'

Description – a very detailed, unattractive image of Betsy Snap is created through:
- adjectives – 'withered, hard-favoured, yellow old woman'
- figurative language – 'connecting them both with the Dissecting Room'.

Actions – Betsy is presented as hard-working, dutiful and obedient:
- 'always employed'
- 'rubbing my uncle's legs' and 'kneeling beside him'
- 'he put his lean grip on the crown of her head' and 'turned her face towards me'.

22. Creating atmosphere

1 (a) Answer extract B
(b) For example: Extract B is the most effective as it uses a clear P-E-E structure and fully explains the connotations of 'prison', 'fortress' and 'stern'.

2 For example: The writer uses the verb 'shivering', which has connotations of fear as well as cold, to emphasise how unpleasant life is in uncle Chill's house. This is further emphasised by the contrasting description of the street as a place where the sun 'did sometimes shine' even in winter, and where 'cheerful faces' passed by. The narrator is described as having a 'heavy heart', which suggests deep sadness, as does the use of the adjectives 'long' and 'low' for the breakfast room.

3 For example: Overall, the writer creates an atmosphere **that is unwelcoming by choosing language that describes the house as cold and unfriendly.**

23. Narrative voice

1 Extract 1: C
Extract 2: A
Extract 3: B

2 Answers could include these key points about the first person narration:
- the narrator's description of the cold and how he is 'shivering' as he comes downstairs suggests that his uncle's house is physically uncomfortable, but also that he is afraid
- 'I carried a heavy heart' shows that the narrator is feeling sad and depressed, which is reinforced by the description of the 'long, low breakfast-room'.

24. Putting it into practice

Paper 1, Question 3 – answers could include these key points:
- overall – build-up of tension using close description of action, together with vivid images of uncontrollable fire and terrified, helpless people
- simile 'like a wild beast from its lair' suggests that the fire is out of control and that the men will be powerless to stop it as it will literally eat them alive
- verbs to suggest people's fear – 'crouched', 'staring', 'wringing'
- vivid image created of dangerous fire – 'gleams and flashes'
- verbs and adverbs show the inactivity of others – 'staring up vacantly', 'clustered'
- description highlights the villagers' despair – 'haggard men' and 'terrified women'
- final image uses strong verbs – 'suffocating, burning, dying'.

25. Rhetorical devices 1

1 For example, four of the following:
- pattern of three – 'polite, quiet and cooperative'
- lists – 'insolent, noisy, crabby, offensive ...'
- alliteration – 'skulking, smoking'
- rhetorical questions – 'But why shocking?'
- colloquial language –'"lost it"', 'whingeing', 'shut the little toads up'.

2 For example (taking colloquial language as an example): ... The writer also uses **colloquial language at the start of the article when she states that the teacher '"lost it"' in class. The writer uses this conversational tone to suggest that the teacher behaved like a teenager. As this phrase is used by young people to describe losing control, it will encourage readers to make a negative judgement about the teacher.**

26. Rhetorical devices 2

1 For example:
'first waves' – the repetition of 'first waves' suggests that the US has always been at the forefront of advances in technology and will continue to be the leader
'we mean'– the writer repeats the phrase 'we mean' to emphasise his confidence that the US will be the country to lead the exploration of space.

2 For example: The phrase 'hostile flag' has connotations of a takeover, whereas 'banner of freedom' suggests that space travel will be a cause for celebration. 'Weapons of mass destruction' is a threatening image and the writer contrasts this with the far more positive idea of 'instruments of knowledge' to suggest that space travel is scientific and will further the progress of mankind.

3 For example:
Hyperbole: the exaggeration in the phrase 'we will have literally reached the stars before midnight tonight' creates a very positive and exciting image about space travel, likening it to romance.
Emotive language: the emotive language in the metaphor 'a new terrifying theater of war' is used to build a frightening picture for the audience of what will happen if space travel is misused.

27. Fact, opinion and expert evidence

1 (a) A
(b) C
(c) B

2 For example: The writer feels that teaching is made very difficult by poorly behaved children.

3 Fact: 'my … 27-stitch scar'.
Opinion: 'supply-teaching hell', '13 is a particularly cruel age'.
Expert evidence: 'I passed two 13-year-old girls. "She looks uglier than ever," said they, laughing merrily.'

4 For example:
Fact: The writer includes the fact about the number of stitches to emphasise the cruelty of the girls given the serious nature of her injury.
Opinion: The writer gives her opinion that supply teaching is 'hell' to reinforce the extent of the challenge faced by teachers.
Expert evidence: The writer's own story about the rude 13-year-old girls makes her view that children are poorly behaved seem believable as it comes from her actual experience of behaviour in schools.

28. Identifying sentence types

1 Sentence A is a single-clause sentence.
Sentence C is a multi-clause sentence (coordinate).
Sentence D is a minor sentence.
Sentence B is a multi-clause sentence (subordinate).

2 For example:
single-clause: 'Her career is now ruined.'
multi-clause (subordinate): 'If she had cried, they would have laughed out loud.'
multi-clause (coordinate): 'But the children were "petrified … burst into tears" and were offered "support".'
minor: 'The pathetic little wets.'

29. Commenting on sentence types

1 For example: The quicker, short, often single-clause sentences at the beginning of the extract suggest an initial atmosphere of tension and fear. The longer, multi-clause sentence slows the extract down and reflects the new sense of calm in the scene being described.

2 For example: The writer starts the paragraph by explaining where and for how long the narrator waited. This is immediately followed by a short, single-clause sentence starting with the word 'still', which creates suspense because **it will leave the reader wanting to know whether Eustacia will return and, if not, what Clym will do next.**
After this short, single-clause sentence, the writer then uses several longer, multi-clause sentences followed by another short, single-clause sentence. This adds to the suspense **as it gives details of Clym's actions, with each additional clause revealing something else about Eustacia's disappearance, like clues in a mystery story. The final short, single-clause sentence adds to the suspense as it acts as a cliffhanger.**

3 For example: The initial multi-clause sentence ends with a question, which draws the reader into the crisis, after which the single-clause sentence 'To follow her was almost impossible' highlights the difficulty Clym faces. The two long, multi-clauses sentences that complete the paragraph show Clym's thought processes, as each clause explores the options open to him.

30. Structure: non-fiction

1 For example: Hanson starts her article by shocking readers with a vivid and detailed description of a teacher who "'lost it'" in class. Readers will want to read on to find out the rest of the story, and to find out how Hanson really feels about teachers.

2 warnings – Hanson wants readers to think carefully about behaviour in the classroom, and the effect this could have on teachers' careers.

3 For example: Initially, Arlidge is scared about the idea of having two electrodes attached to his head. This is implied in the phrase 'pumping electricity straight into my brain'. However, when he actually tries the electrodes, his tone changes. **This is signalled in the short sentence 'And then something remarkable happens', which draws attention to a shift in his reaction to what is happening. This is then followed by two longer sentences, creating a positive picture of 'waves gently flowing', which reflect his calmer state of mind. The verb 'slump' contrasts with the earlier verb 'pumping' and suggests a complete change in mood.**

31. Structure: fiction

1 The words 'fearful' and 'confessing' in the lines above suggest that the narrator knows his uncle will **disapprove of the engagement. This suggests to the reader that a disagreement will follow and that uncle Chill is likely to react badly to the news.**

2 For example: The writer describes Eustacia's actions in detail as it shows how carefully and methodically she prepares for her journey. For instance, she is shown lighting her candle and then in the same sentence is shown 'extinguishing the light'. This also emphasises how careful she is to avoid discovery. The writer shows her 'pausing at the door' at the end of the paragraph as the rain is 'threatening to come on heavily'. This builds tension as it suggests that the rain will be a metaphor for the journey she is about to take.

3 Answers should include comments about how the closely described detail in the short extract draws out the action and builds tension by showing her careful preparations, with the final paragraph acting as a climax to the tension as she realises that she is, in fact, not prepared enough for the reality of her situation.

32. Putting it into practice

Paper 1, Question 3 – answers could include these key points:

- starts with reference to time, which is critical – 'It would be a quarter of an hour'
- initial, shorter sentences lay out the facts and reflect the narrator's thought processes
- multi-clause sentence starting 'In defiance of my own reason …' suggests possible reasons for action
- questions used to explore options for action reflect the narrator's desperation to find a way to save the trapped man
- multi-clause sentence starting 'I knew the strength of the heavy lock …' lists the reasons why a rescue will be very difficult, reinforced by the repetition of 'I knew'.

33. Putting it into practice

Paper 2, Question 3 – answers could include the following key points.

Language:

- informal phrases create a personal tone – e.g. 'hit a certain age', 'in a flash', 'screwed on tight'
- colloquial language is used to show the mother can relate to her daughter's situation – e.g. 'doesn't get it', 'total disaster'
- repetition for emphasis – e.g. 'barmy old dinosaur', 'I am proud to call you my daughter', 'it's not real life', 'dangerous', 'please', 'think about it'
- hyperbole creates humour, which makes the mother's advice more likely to be followed – e.g. 'barmy old dinosaur', 'with a cable and everything'
- adjectives and adverbs emphasise how dangerous sexting can appear to others – e.g. 'seductively', 'alluring', 'provocative'
- contrasts – e.g, 'For you, a world without social media ... For me, it would make my job ... easier' – emphasise how much the mother understands in spite of her concerns.

Structure:

- starts with introductory one-sentence paragraph ending in 'scenario', which will intrigue the reader
- first half of letter outlines the dangers of social media, then the minor sentence 'A dangerous one' and the one-sentence paragraph that follows change the tone and refocus the second half of the letter on advice
- advice and explanation paragraphs contain longer sentences with several clauses, which suggests the information is reliable and well thought out
- letter ends on a loving note and with a kiss.

34. Handling two texts

1 separate
2 Assessment objective 3
3 (a) Paper 2
(b) Question 7 (b)
(c) Question 7 (a)
(d) Question 7 (a)
(e) Question 7 (b)
(f) Question 7 (b)
(g) Question 7 (a)

35. Selecting evidence for synthesis

1 'OK, you try teaching 13-year-olds': Answer provided on page 35.
Bad Blood: 'sat surveying us, tapping his pointer gently in the palm of his left hand'.
2 What <u>similarities</u> are there between the <u>risky behaviours</u> of the <u>young people</u>?
3 Extract (a) i and Extract (b) i

36. Synthesising evidence

1 Similarly, likewise, both writers feel, in the same way, both texts suggest
2 For example: You should use adverbials and linking phrases in your synthesis to link together the similarities you find between the two texts.
3 (a) Overview C
(b) For example: Overview C shows an understanding of the specific similarity between the two texts.
4 Answers should use suitable adverbials and linking phrases, and start with the overview identified in Question 3 (a) above. They could use the evidence identified for Question 3 on page 35.
For example: Both texts suggest that young people take risks that cause their parents to worry. For instance, Whitton writes about how dangerous it is to 'press 'send' on a provocative image'. Similarly, James writes about dangerous behaviour that caused his mother worry, such as when he organised cycling competitions that went on 'endlessly against the clock'.

37. Looking closely at language

1 'bonkers' – Answer provided on page 37.
'gizmos' – means 'modern gadgets', an informal term with trendy connotations.
'wearable kit' – suggests fashionable and essential, rather than functional, items.
2 For example: The colloquial language of 'bonkers', meaning 'mad' or 'crazy', creates an informal tone with positive connotations. The word 'gizmos' and the phrase 'wearable kit' both suggest fashionable items rather than functional ones, which creates the impression that the writer does not really take the new technology seriously.
3 For example: The three subordinate clauses contain more factual information about the purpose of the devices, such as 'monitoring our blood pressure'. This gives the sentence a more serious and scientific tone.
4 (a) For example: The repetition of 'tap into' makes changing the way we feel sound simple.
(b) For example: The long, multi-clause sentence that follows the repetition in the four short, single clause sentences creates a reassuring effect, which persuades the reader that this is something they might want to try.

38. Planning to compare

1 Completed plans should include example quotations and explanations, as per the Extract 2 examples below.
Tone:
- sarcastic, angry: for example, 'supply-teaching hell' makes writer's viewpoint clear.

Rhetorical devices/language:
- hyperbole: for example, 'dribbling glue' paints a negative view of students
- anecdote: for example, 'In my first year's teaching ...' draws the reader in and shows the writer is drawing on personal experience, which persuades the reader to believe her.

Sentences: long, multi-clause sentences emphasise how difficult teaching is.

39. Comparing ideas and perspectives

1 Both texts start by expressing ideas about **the risks taken by young people and the way parents feel about their children's risky behaviour.**
2 For example: In contrast, James describes how his mother showed little or no sympathy for her son's behaviour as she used physical punishment. The extent of her distress is obvious; she even told her son she was struggling by saying he was 'more than she could cope with', which makes her difficulties sound serious.
3 For example: Both texts start by expressing ideas about the risks taken by young people and the way parents feel about their children's risky behaviour. Whitton's letter suggests that she is sympathetic to the risks taken by young people but is also aware of the dangers of sending 'a provocative image'. In contrast, James describes how his mother used physical punishment in response to his behaviour, which was 'more than she could cope with'. Whitton's supportive perspective

continues through to the loving kiss. Similarly, James's perspective remains light-hearted throughout as he recalls his 'exploits' in spite of his mother's 'tears'.

40. Answering a comparison question

1 Answers should:
- compare the language in the two texts
- focus on the effect of the writer's language choices
- support key points with evidence and explanation/ analysis.

41. Putting it into practice

Answers could include the following key points.
'Dear daughter':
- ideas about risky behaviour – sharing 'provocative' images on social media – which worry the mother
- writer concerned about daughter, serious parental perspective despite informal tone and humour
- informal tone helps to deliver the warning in a friendly way – 'hit a certain age', 'in a flash', 'screwed on tight'
- humour created through hyperbole, to engage her daughter with the dangers – 'barmy old dinosaur'
- adjectives and adverbs used to emphasise danger – 'seductively', 'alluring', 'provocative'
- structure – first half outlines the dangers of social media, then the minor sentence 'A dangerous one' and the one-sentence paragraph that follows change the tone and refocus the second half of the letter on advice
- letter ends on loving note and with a kiss.

Unreliable Memoirs:
- ideas about risky behaviour – 'exploits' upset his mother
- writer intending to entertain, gives child's perspective on behaviour
- informal tone created through anecdotes – 'Once when'
- humour created through images – 'fall dramatically into the bush and disappear'
- verbs used to emphasise the danger – 'circulating', 'plunge', 'fall', 'disappear'
- structured as several anecdotes that increase in danger
- sense of knowing his behaviour was wrong – 'hiding', 'guilt and fear'.

42. Evaluating a text

1 summarise

2 (a) False
(b) True
(c) True
(d) Answer provided on page 42.
(e) False
(f) True

3 All four aspects may not be relevant to a text; for instance, 'settings' may not apply to a non-fiction text.

4 A iii; B iv; C ii; D i
(b) (Ideas) What the writer thinks or believes.

5 Paper 1, Question 4:
How long to spend on answer: about 30 minutes
Focus of question: bravery of the narrator
I'll need to look at: an effect that is created in the extract.
Paper 2, Question 6:
How long to spend on answer: about 15 minutes
Focus of question: descriptions of youthful exploits
I'll need to look at: one specific aspect of the extract.

43. Evaluating a text: fiction

1 For example: My life at my uncle Chill's was of a spare dull kind, <u>and my garret chamber was as dull, and bare, and cold, as an upper prison room in some stern northern fortress</u>. But, having Christiana's love, I wanted nothing upon earth. I would not have changed my lot with any human being. …
As I came down-stairs next morning, shivering in the cold December air; <u>colder in my uncle's unwarmed house</u> than in the street, where the <u>winter sun did sometimes shine</u>, and which was at all events <u>enlivened by cheerful faces and voices passing along</u>; I carried a heavy heart towards the <u>long, low breakfast-room</u> in which my uncle sat.

2 For example: The setting builds sympathy for the narrator as it is presented by the writer as harsh. **Firstly, the narrator is presented as trapped inside the house, with his own room described as a 'garret' that is like a 'prison room' in a 'fortress'. The next paragraph builds on this harsh image as it goes on to describe the downstairs part of the house, which is no better than his room as it is colder than the street outside. Sympathy for the narrator builds further as the street outside is contrasted to the cold interior and described as 'enlivened' by 'cheerful' people, whereas the narrator has to enter a 'long, low' room.**

3 Events could include:
- the narrator writing a letter to his uncle
- the narrator greeting his uncle
- uncle Chill hitting the narrator with his stick
- uncle Chill shouting at the narrator and calling him names.

4 For example: The writer builds sympathy for the narrator through the events described in the extract. For example, out of fear of his uncle, the narrator writes the news of his engagement in a letter to him. The fact that he hands the letter to his uncle 'on going to bed' suggests that he wants to avoid his uncle's immediate reaction. This sense of fear is continued the next morning and the reader sympathises with the narrator as he goes to greet his uncle with 'a heavy heart'. The physical and verbal abuse he then suffers at the hands of his uncle who 'made a blow' at him increases the reader's sympathy for the narrator even more.

44. Evaluating a text: non-fiction

1 For example:
'Such catastrophes distressed my mother', 'Other exploits broke her heart' – Idea: distress/worry of mother.
'Once when she was out shopping' – Idea: getting up to mischief while parents are absent
'Passing boys noticed what I was up to' – Idea: the narrator is leading other boys astray.

2 For example:
I organised a spectacular finish in which the riders had to <u>plunge into my mother's prize privet hedge.</u> The idea was for the bike's front wheel to lodge in the thick privet and the rider to <u>fall dramatically into the bush and disappear.</u> It became harder and harder to disappear as the <u>privet became more and more reduced to ruins.</u>

3 For example:
- James sets up the 'complicated circuit' while his mother is out
- boys join in and the circuit gets more dangerous
- James's mother returns and punishes him
- James and his friends 'bomb' and break his bed.

4 For example: James entertains the reader with detailed and humorous descriptions of his youthful exploits. His tone is light-hearted and the humour as he describes plunging into his mother's 'prize privet hedge' and the aim to 'fall dramatically into the bush and disappear', for example, allows the reader to picture the scene from a comic perspective. The level of detail as James recalls one event after another also helps to build a sense of climax as the 'complicated circuit' becomes more dangerous. This is entertaining as we ask ourselves what will happen next.

45. Putting it into practice

Answers could include the following key points.

Events – described in detail, which draws out suspense; for example:

- Clym's actions are described in detail, from 'waiting nearly five minutes', through 'hastily putting on his clothes', to checking the front door
- Eustacia's actions are also described in detail, from her preparations ('lighted her candle', 'extinguishing the light again') to opening her umbrella and, finally, her realisation that she has no money.

Setting – described in detail, which also builds suspense; for example:

- Eustacia's room with the 'impression of her form' on the bed, which has not been slept in
- the description of the heath at night, which highlights the dangers of Eustacia's 'flight' and builds suspense as finding her is presented as 'a hopeless task'
- the night sky, which is described in detail as 'funereal' with nothing visible except one light, suggesting that Eustacia may not survive
- nature around the pool, which is described in threatening detail – 'oozing lumps of fleshy fungi' and 'rotten liver and lungs'.

Ideas – the idea of running away in secret adds to the suspense.

46. Putting it into practice

Answers could include the following key points.

Ideas – the main idea is how far man has progressed:

- first two paragraphs 'condense' man's 'recorded history' into a 'half-century' to emphasise the speed of progress
- pace of history is 'breathtaking' but comes with risk from 'high costs and hardships'
- the US needs to lead the 'race for space'
- space needs to be a place of knowledge, a 'sea of peace' not a 'terrifying theater of war'
- space can be a place of 'peaceful cooperation'
- mankind takes on challenges despite them being hard.

Theme – speech is very persuasive and positive, with space travel described as an adventure:

- space travel is described as exciting – 'we will have literally reached the stars before midnight tonight' and 'one of the great adventures of all time'
- speech appeals to the patriotism of the audience – they cannot stay behind in the 'race for space'
- conquering space is described as an adventure – 'set sail on this new sea'
- space conquest 'deserves the best of all mankind'.

SECTION B: WRITING

47. Writing questions: an overview

1 (a) Paper 1
(b) Paper 2
(c) Paper 2
(d) Both
(e) Both

2 (a) Both
(b) AO6
(c) AO6
(d) AO5

3 For example:
Assessment objective 5 (a) – Write fluently and engagingly using appropriate techniques to suit a variety of audiences, purposes and styles.
Assessment objective 5 (b) – Arrange **ideas effectively using appropriate techniques to ensure the text is clear.**
Assessment objective 6 – Use a wide selection of words in a range of sentence styles, and accurate spelling and punctuation throughout.

48. Writing questions: Paper 1

1 (a) False
(b) True
(c) True
(d) True

2 This phrase should be circled: 'Your response could be real or imagined.'

3 'may'

4 Planning your answer: 10 minutes
Writing your answer: 30 minutes
Checking and proofreading your answer: 5 minutes

49. Writing questions: Paper 2

1 Answer given on page 49.
intended to achieve a specific purpose / ~~amusing and light-hearted~~
~~entertaining and humorous~~ / serious, with humour only if appropriate to audience
for a specific audience / ~~suitable for all ages~~
Answer given on page 49.

2 (a) These words should be circled: 'Headteacher/ Principal'
(b) This word should be circled in Question 8: 'report'. This word should be circled in Question 9: 'article'.
(c) These words should be circled in Question 8: 'suggesting ways in which the school could encourage healthy eating'.
These words should be circled in Question 9: 'exploring the idea'.

3

	Start writing at 11.00 am
Planning your answer	11.00 – 11.10 am
Writing your answer	11.10 – 11.40 am
Checking and proofreading your answer	11.40 – 11.45 am

50. Writing for a purpose: imaginative

1 For example:

see:	a kaleidoscope of brilliant colours
hear:	screeching crowds on the rollercoasters
smell:	answer provided on page 50
touch:	the excited grip of my sister's warm hand
taste:	syrupy sweet candy-floss

2 For example: My face lit up with a wide smile and **my excitement mounted as I pushed through the crowds and stole my first glimpse of the brightly lit rides.**

3 For example:
Simile: colours as bright and dazzling as a firework display
Metaphor: rides towering over us
Personification: the darkness swallowed us as our ride on the ghost train began

4 Answers should:
- use the senses
- include examples of figurative language
- include examples of carefully chosen language
- use verbs that show rather than tell
- maintain one narrative voice throughout.

For example: My face lit up with a wide smile and my excitement mounted as I pushed through the crowds and stole my first glimpse of the brightly lit rides. A kaleidoscope of colours as bright and dazzling as a firework display met my eager eyes and, inhaling deeply, I could almost taste the syrupy sweet candy-floss on sale nearby. I squeezed my sister's hand and grinned.

51. Writing for a purpose: inform, explain, review

1 Example subheadings could include:
- What is already on offer
- New services for teenagers
- Teenager-friendly opening times
- Providing a study zone for teenagers

in addition to the answer provided on page 51.

2 Remember that you can make facts and statistics up, as long as they are believable. For example:
- more than 50 per cent of teenagers have not considered using the local library for study
- over three-quarters of teenagers said that they might use the local library if facilities were improved
- opening times extended to 7 pm would attract students after school hours
- 95 per cent of all teenagers said that they would be more likely to use the library if there was a special study zone.

3 Answers might include subheadings and should include examples of facts and statistics. The tone of the writing should be formal. For example: The local library currently works hard to offer a broad and flexible service. Nonetheless, more than half of local teenagers have not considered using the facilities for study purposes. This suggests that, while the library's efforts to attract the attention of other sections of society are successful, it is currently failing to appeal to those aged 18 and under.

52. Writing for a purpose: argue and persuade

1 Examples of points that **agree** with the idea could include: people spend hours on the internet; like other addictive drugs, people's use increases the more they use it, becoming more and more dependent; people denied access can suffer cravings.
Examples of points that **disagree** with the idea could include: the time people spend on the internet shows how useful it is; it does not cause physical harm; using the internet is no different to reading a book or meeting friends, except it is onscreen.

2 Answers will vary. Remember that you can make evidence up, as long as it is believable. For example:
Agree – Point: people spend hours on the internet; Evidence: 75 per cent of all teenagers admit to spending at least two hours online every day.
Disagree – Point: using the internet is no different to reading a book or meeting friends, except it is onscreen; Evidence: research conducted by Professor Nett and his team show that people who interact online rather than face-to-face have an equally healthy social life.

3 For example:
Agree – Some people might feel **that we spend too much time on the internet.** However, **it is clear from the number of hours that people spend online on a daily basis that the internet is an invaluable resource in the modern age.**
Disagree – Some people might feel **that the internet is not a danger as it does not cause physical harm.** However, **recent studies clearly show a rise in back, neck and wrist injuries resulting from extended periods in front of the screen and over-use of the mouse.**

4 For example (rhetorical device: list, as underlined): Some people might feel **that the internet is not a danger as it does not cause physical harm.** However, **recent studies clearly show a rise in the numbers of internet users suffering from <u>back pain, repetitive strain injury in the wrist and forearm, blurred vision and poor concentration</u>.**

53. Writing for an audience

1 For example: The audience is likely to be **adults of both genders, probably those aged over 25, although younger people may read the article as it concerns them.**

2 Sentence B – The tone and vocabulary in this sentence are formal, which is appropriate for a national newspaper article whose audience is mainly adults.

3 Answers should be appropriate for a teenage audience, and may include some informal language although non-Standard English, including slang and texting language, should be avoided. A variety of sentence structures and a wide vocabulary should also be used. For example: ... increasing the amount of green vegetables you eat is a good starting point. **To begin with, while green, leafy vegetables may not appeal to your taste buds, they are nonetheless packed with fibre, vitamins and minerals. Their health benefits are widely acknowledged: apart from great skin and bundles of energy, these greens are thought to help protect you from diseases like diabetes, and possibly even cancer.**

54. Putting it into practice

1 Planning time: 10 minutes
Writing time: 30 minutes
Checking time: 5 minutes
Form: prose
Narrative voice: answer will vary, but the narrative voice isn't specified in the question, so the choice is open.

2 Examples of language techniques will vary, but might include: using the senses, figurative language.

55. Putting it into practice

1 For example:

	Question 8	Question 9
Timing	Plan: 10 minutes Write: 30 minutes Check: 5 minutes	Plan: 10 minutes Write: 30 minutes Check: 5 minutes
Topic	Facilities at sports centre	Dogs in local park
Form	Review	Article
Audience	Adults, but younger people may read	Adults, but younger people may read
Purpose	To inform	To argue and persuade
Key features	Subheading, rating, engaging opening paragraph, detailed paragraphs, some figurative language	Key points with evidence, such as facts and statistics or expert opinions, counter-arguments, rhetorical questions

56. Form: articles and reviews

1 Answers will vary and should be suitable for an adult audience. For example: Clampdown on kids' chaos.

2 Answers will vary and should be suitable for an adult audience. For example: Is a 9 pm curfew the only way to control our teenagers?

3 Answers will vary and should be suitable for an adult audience. For example: 'The idea of a curfew is fundamentally flawed,' argues John Jones, father of two. 'It may help with the odd troublemaker, but it will also have a serious effect on the social lives of the vast majority of well-behaved teenagers.'

4 (The television programme on which this guided question is based is *I'm A Celebrity ... Get Me Out Of Here!*) Answers should include a further two or three sentences containing figurative devices or language techniques, such as use of the senses, simile, metaphor and personification. For example:
In the jungle, the skies darken, the heavens open and a talentless celebrity nobody has ever heard of chokes on a handful of live maggots. My favourite television programme is like **an addictive smoothie – a tangy fusion of everything we like to gossip about and squeal at. The jungle setting pulls us in as we wonder how we would cope with the cramped conditions, the cacophony of camp life and the lack of a decent power shower. And, as the latest celebrity reaches for a witchetty grub, our stomachs churn in delight and horror.**

57. Form: letters and reports

1 (a) True
(b) True
(c) False (you should use 'Yours faithfully' if you have used 'Dear Sir/Madam')
(d) True

2 For example:
Headline: Youth Councils
Opening sentence: Many councils across the UK and Europe have set up youth councils and have found them to be an effective way to access the views of young people.

3 For example:
(a) Firstly, I would suggest **setting up a Facebook page, as well as using other popular forms of social media, such as Twitter. Young people are used to communicating in this way and are therefore more likely to respond through these channels.**
(b) **I would also recommend visiting schools and colleges to talk to students directly. This would give students a deeper understanding of why a youth council is important and will encourage them to get involved.**

58. Form: information guides

1 For example:
(a) Find it, see it, love it!
(b) What's going on and where to find it.
(c) What's on, Sherlock?

2 For example: 'Find it, see it, love it!' would be most effective for a teenage audience because the pattern of three and the repetition of 'it' make it straight to the point as well as eye-catching.

3 For example:
(a) Answer provided on page 58.
(b) Getting from A to B
(c) Eat, drink, enjoy

4 For example:
Read on to find out:
- what's on and where it is
- how to get around
- where to find the best food
- what not to miss.

Note that answers to Questions 1, 3 and 4 should use language and a tone that is suitable for a teenage audience – punchy, and possibly with some informal language but still in Standard English.

59. Putting it into practice

Answers should be suitable for an adult audience, be written in a formal tone, and could include:
- Dear ...
- A subject line
- key points
- evidence, e.g. facts or statistics
- counter-arguments
- rhetorical devices
- adverbials to signpost the path through points made
- a conclusion
- Yours ...

60. Prose: an overview

1 (a) True
(b) True
(c) False

2 This option should be ticked: c

3 For example: Prose is continuous, paragraphed writing.

4 Narrative: Extract C
Description: Extract A
Monologue: Extract B

61. Ideas and planning: imaginative

1 Either of the two questions could be chosen.

2 Answers will vary depending on the option chosen in Question 1, but all plans should answer key questions about the characters (e.g. who is there, what they are like) and the action (e.g. what is happening, what has happened already).

3 Details added should develop the idea and include examples of imaginative writing techniques, such as figurative devices and use of the senses. For example, for Question 6: describe the journey, personification of aeroplane – whisks us away.

62. Structure: imaginative

1 Answers will vary but all should:
- complete the narrative structure with a balanced amount of detail for each stage
- include ideas about imaginative writing techniques.

For example:
Exposition: Relaxing in front of fire on windy winter day. Door bells rings. I answer – it is my long-lost sister. Use dialogue **to introduce her character.**
Rising action: **In kitchen, making tea – use senses. Sister starts to tell me where she's been all these years. Depict sister – show not tell; simile/metaphor to describe her manner.**
Climax: **Reveals she's been living in Peru, where she set up an organisation to help the poor; personification to express my surprise.**
Falling action: **She explains her project and its aims; use vivid vocabulary to picture the setting.**
Resolution: **She invites me to go out there for the summer to help with her work; action verbs.**

2 As for Question 1. Answers should adapt the answer to Question 1 and follow the flashback structure given.
For example:
Climax: Reveals she's been living in Peru, where she set up an organisation to help the poor; personification to express my surprise.
Exposition: Relaxing in front of fire on windy winter day. Door bells rings. I answer – it is my long-lost sister. Use dialogue to introduce her character.
Rising action: In kitchen, making tea – use senses. Sister starts to tell me where she's been all these years. Depict sister – show not tell; simile/metaphor to describe her manner.
Return to climax: Sister telling me about Peru.
Falling action: She explains her project and its aims; use vivid vocabulary to picture the setting.
Resolution: She invites me to go out there for the summer to help with her work; action verbs.

63. Beginnings and endings: imaginative

1 Beginnings should not over-use dialogue and should contain appropriate figurative devices and language techniques. For example, for 'Conflict or danger': The envelope burned in my hand. To open it was, I knew, to enter a different world where I would never be completely safe again. My heart thundered in my chest and my blood boiled past my ears.

2 Answers will vary depending on the opening chosen from Question 1. For example, for 'Conflict or danger': The tone of my ending will be one of happy relief. The contents of the letter will not be as bad as the narrator fears but will teach them a lesson about prying into secrets.

3 As for Question 2. Answers should reflect the tone decided on in Question 2. For example, for 'Conflict or danger':
(a) I sat down and breathed a long, deep sigh of relief.
(b) I knew I had been lucky this time and I knew I would never make the same mistake again.
(c) I took a breath and smiled, and, as I smiled, the furrows in my brow finally eased.

64. Putting it into practice

1 Plans should include:
- some form of five-part narrative structure, for example, a spider diagram
- ideas for the beginning/ending
- details of narrative voice and imaginative writing techniques to be used.

65. Ideas and planning: inform, explain, review

1 Plans should include:
- a title
- an introduction and a conclusion
- a subheading and a rating
- an opening paragraph
- three or four sequenced key points
- a range of supporting details.

66. Ideas and planning: argue and persuade

1 Plans should include:
- an introduction and a conclusion
- three sequenced key points
- supporting evidence
- a counter-argument.

67. Openings: transactional

1 For example:
Using a rhetorical question – Is prison the answer to serious crime?
Making a bold or controversial statement – Prison has never been less effective in preventing serious crime.
With a relevant quotation – 'Prison saved me. It turned my life around.'
With a shocking or surprising fact or statistic – No less than 58% of offenders sentenced to less than a year in prison go on to reoffend.
With a short, relevant, interesting anecdote – Answer provided on page 67.

2 Answers will vary but all should:
- introduce the topic
- engage the reader
- include one or two of the suggested approaches from Question 1.

68. Conclusions: transactional

1 For example:
End on a vivid image – As the colossal prison door swings shut behind yet another serial offender, so too does the window of opportunity to make a real change.
End on a warning – If alternatives to prison sentences are not found soon, serious crime rates will only continue to rise.
End on a happy note – Crime may not pay, but with serious crime rates on the decrease, sending offenders to prison certainly does.
End on a thought-provoking question. Answer provided on page 68.
End on a 'call to action' – We must call on the government to think again about their approach to prison sentences. Now is the time for change.
Refer back to introduction – So, prison is not the whole answer to serious crime, but it is a vital part of the solution.

2 Answers will vary but all should include one or two of the suggested approaches from Question 1.

69. Putting it into practice

1 Plans should include:
- an engaging title
- a subheading
- a rating
- an idea for an engaging opening paragraph
- ideas for about three sequenced paragraphs, with details of figurative language to be used
- an idea for the conclusion.

70. Paragraphing for effect

1 Point: When students choose …
Evidence: I chose my GCSEs …
Explain: Neither of these reasons …

2 For example:
Point: The careers advice currently available to students is inadequate.
Evidence: Students make poor choices about which subjects to continue to study.
Explain: Students find themselves badly prepared or unable to pursue the career that best suits them.

3 For example: While schools and colleges do offer some careers advice to students, the advice is frequently inadequate, failing to outline clearly all possible career paths students may wish to follow. This is clear in the poor choices students make about which subjects to continue studying, which often do not support their ideal career. As a result, students find themselves badly prepared or unable to pursue the career they are best suited to, a situation which could be prevented with more and improved careers advice.

4 Point: While schools and colleges …
Evidence: This is clear in the poor choices …
Explain: As a result …

71. Linking ideas

1

Adding an idea	Furthermore…	Moreover…
Explaining	Consequently	Therefore
Illustrating	For example	For instance
Emphasising	In particular	Significantly
Comparing	In the same way	Similarly
Contrasting	However	On the other hand

2 Extract 1 examples: For example …; therefore …
Extract 2 examples: Moreover … ; Significantly …; … for instance …

3 Answers will vary but all should use a P-E-E structure and feature a range of adverbials. For example: Exams cannot give a fair and accurate picture of a student's real abilities as too much is dependent on the day of the exam and how the student is feeling on that particular day. For instance, a student might be highly competent and have worked hard to prepare for the exam. However, they may also have had a sleepless night or be struggling with an illness on the day of the exam, which may lead to poorer marks than they might otherwise have attained. Consequently, exams are not only an unrepresentative but also an unfair means of assessing a student's ability.

72. Putting it into practice

Answers should include:

- appropriate features for audience, purpose and form
- well-structured and sequenced paragraphs, with one main point or idea per paragraph
- a range of adverbials to link paragraphs and guide the reader.

73. Vocabulary for effect: synonyms

1 For example:
Students: pupils, exam candidates, learners
Improve: develop, enhance, extend
Learning: achievement, attainment, skills
Doing: completing, achieving, carrying out, performing

2 For example:
Embarrassed: Answer provided on page 73.
Upset: concerned, worried, alarmed
Scream: yell, shriek, shout
Moment: occasion, time, situation
Annoyed: aggravated, agitated, distressed

3 Answers will vary but all should include some of the synonyms from Question 2. For example: On that day, on that occasion, I was mortified. I could have yelled or shouted, agitated as I was, but my sense of humiliation was total. I could barely manage a whisper. I tried to speak. Nothing. Alarmed at what they might be thinking, I took a deep breath and tried again.

74. Vocabulary for effect: argue and persuade

1 For example:
A – Answer provided on page 74.
B – 'use too many' could be replaced by: devour, fritter
'not have enough food' could be replaced by: starve
C – 'filled with' could be replaced by: dominated by, ruled by
'not like' could be replaced by: hate, detest
'cannot do much about it' could be replaced by: are powerless to change it

2 For example:
(a) The word 'roar' suggests a lion and has connotations of loudness, anger, aggression and dominance. This would suggest that some parents are determined to fight the plans and win.
(b) The word 'howl' suggests loudness, though perhaps a loudness that is ineffective, which creates the impression that the parents are protesting but that the plans will go ahead.
(c) The word 'whimper' suggests weakness and that the parents do not present a real opposition to the school's plans.

3 Answers will vary but all should consist of two sentences and include vocabulary chosen for its impact and connotations. For example: There are those who feel that social networking is a colossal waste of time, squandering the precious hours we might otherwise lavish on worthier pursuits. Yet, for many, social networks are a lifeline, a vital connection with those on whose friendship and support they rely.

75. Language for different effects 1

1 A Rhetorical question
B Answer provided on page 75.
C Contrast, list
D Contrast
E Rhetorical question
F Repetition

2 Answers will vary but all should consist of four short extracts. Each extract should use one or more of the language techniques explored in Question 1. For example:
Contrast: Furry animals often look cute and cuddly nestled into small cages, but they can turn surprisingly nasty and dangerous when taken out.
Rhetorical question: Would you like to spend your life trapped in a space the size of a small bedroom?
Repetition: Animals need space, animals need air and even small animals deserve freedom.
List: Before you buy a cage for your pet, make sure it is the right size and remember that it will need food, bedding, water, some shade and perhaps even a nesting area.

76. Language for different effects 2

1 A Hyperbole, alliteration
B Direct address (and a rhetorical question)
C Alliteration, pattern of three
D Hyperbole
E Pattern of three
F Direct address

2 Answers will vary but all should consist of four short extracts. Each extract should use one or more of the language techniques explored in Question 1. For example:
Direct address: Do you really believe that our schools, the centres of learning that open for us so many doors of opportunity and of possibility, can be considered cruel?
Pattern of three: School is vital in teaching us to ask questions, seek answers and use our understanding to make the world a better place.
Alliteration: The cruelty of our crusty and crumbling school regime is designed to cripple the imagination and crush the soul.
Hyperbole: School is undoubtedly the cruellest and most confining form of imprisonment and torture found in the world today.

77. Language for different effects 3

1 A Personification
B Metaphor
C Simile
D Answer provided on page 77.
E Metaphor
F Personification

2 Answers will vary but all should consist of four short extracts. Each extract should use one of the figurative devices explored in Question 1. For example:
Simile: The layers of dust that covered it were thick and white, like a heavy blanket of fresh snow.
Metaphor: The knowledge of what I'd found was a lead weight around my ankles, and I dragged myself away to think.
Personification: Lying just out of reach of my outstretched fingers, the glistening jewel teased me from the shadows.

78. Using the senses

1 Any two of the extracts should be circled, according to personal choice.

2 Answers will vary according to the extracts chosen in Question 1, but explanations should reflect the 'show not tell' technique of using the senses.

3 Answers will vary but all should:
- consist of one paragraph
- use at least three of the senses and the 'show not tell' technique
- include examples of figurative language such as similes, metaphors and personification.

For example: My skin prickled. Again the whining creak of the stair pierced the silence. I froze, half squatting, half kneeling on the icy slabs. As dark as pitch, the house waited and I, a frightened animal, held my breath.

79. Narrative voice

1 A – first person
B – Answer provided on page 79.
C – first person
D – third person

2 Answers will vary but all should consist of two possible openings. Each opening should:
- consist of one or two sentences
- use a different narrative voice.

For example: I opened the door to discarded food, bottles, cans, clothes and even parts of a bicycle, all strewn haphazardly over the filthy carpet. As I crunched what looked distinctly like part of my mother's best dinner service under my foot, I realised the time had come to take a stand.

80. Putting it into practice

Answers should include examples of:
- language appropriate to form, purpose and audience
- language chosen for effect
- figurative devices
- language techniques, e.g. rhetorical questions, pattern of three, etc.

81. Putting it into practice

Answers should include:
- language appropriate to audience
- ambitious and effective language choices
- a range of language techniques, including figurative devices
- a consistent narrative voice.

82. Sentence variety 1

1 Sentence (a): B (multi-clause sentence with a subordinate clause); it has two clauses, one of which is subordinate, linked with *because*.
Sentence (b): E (minor sentence); it has no verb.
Sentence (c): C (multi-clause sentence with a coordinate clause); it has an equal pair of clauses, linked with *but*.
Sentence (d): Answer provided on page 82.
Sentence (e): D (multi-clause sentence with a relative clause); the clause introduced by the relative pronoun *which*, is separated from the main clause with commas.

2 For example: Professional footballers are possibly the worst 'fakers'. With just one tap from another player they fall over, dive to the ground or occasionally fly. They always start screaming because it shows they are seriously injured. They say it was a foul. They demand a free kick. Ridiculous.

83. Sentence variety 2

1 For example:
(a) A pronoun – Answer provided on page 83.
(b) An article – The big city with its bright lights and busy sounds is without a doubt the place for me.
(c) A preposition – Between the closely stacked tower blocks, you can just make out the occasional grey of the Thames.
(d) An -ing word (or present participle) – Crawling around the congested ring road in the sultry summer heat, I dream of country air and open spaces.
(e) An adjective – Slow is not a word for the big city, where speed is everything.
(f) An adverb – Happily, my flat is down a quiet side road and so the sounds of the city are subdued.
(g) A conjunctive – Although I spent my childhood on a farm, city life suits me surprisingly well.

2 Answers will vary but all should aim to:
- include all seven different types of sentence opener from Question 1
- use a different word to start each sentence.

For example: **I** grew up in a tiny village in the middle of nowhere. **Although**, after such quiet beginnings, I was attracted by the hustle and bustle of city life, I know now that my heart belongs in the country. **The** city, with its bright lights and busy sounds, is suffocating to me. **Between** the closely stacked tower blocks, I peer in vain for a glimpse of the river and the hills, and only occasionally am I rewarded. **Walking** home after work last night, I raised my head to the stars of the winter sky and imagined myself at home, where the only hurry is in the current of the stream that runs through our meadow. **Slow** is not a word for the big city. **Unexpectedly**, however, as I raised my head, something wonderful happened.

84. Sentences for different effects

1 The effect of the long sentence is that it emphasises the chain of events, and builds tension as the situation worsens. The effect of the short sentence is that it brings the scene to an abrupt end, focusing on the narrator's horror.

2 The first sentence emphasises **'her' unsympathetic reaction. The second sentence emphasis the long walk home.**
Note that the information the writer wants to emphasise usually comes at the end of the sentence.

3 Answers will vary but all should aim to include a:
- long, multi-clause sentence followed by a short, single-clause sentence
- sentence structured to give specific emphasis.

For example: Just for a moment, imagine that you have to face each day with a disability or a life-limiting condition, that each day presents a risk of exploitation or violence, or that you feel isolated, alone and are vulnerable. Imagine you are a child in need. Children in Need is a wonderful charity through which you and I, our friends and families, and our neighbours and neighbourhoods, can make a difference.

85. Putting it into practice

Answers should include examples of:
- a range of sentence types
- sentences beginning in a range of different ways
- sentences structured for effect.

86. Ending a sentence

1 At the end of a sentence
2 At the end of a question
3 (a) Answer provided on page 86.
(b) Avoid using them for anything other than an exclamation.
(c) Avoid using two or more exclamation marks in a row.
4 Sentence A: Incorrect. This is a comma splice: two sentences are joined with a comma; they should be separated with a full stop or joined with a conjunction.
Sentence B: Correct. The two sentences are separated with a full stop.
Sentence C: Correct. The two sentences are joined with a conjunction.
5 There are eight mistakes in total in the original, including the unnecessary exclamation marks at the end of the title.
<u>A Change of Heart</u>**[1]**
*I braced myself for a confrontation.***[2]** *She was looking at me like she knew I had something to say and she didn't want to hear it. My heart began to race and a strange throbbing pain pulsed in my forehead. How could I say it?***[3]** *How could I tell her what I was thinking without upsetting her?***[4]**
*She knew something was coming.***[5]** *Tears were welling up in her dark brown eyes and her bottom lip was starting to quiver. I didn't feel much better than she did.***[6]** *My stomach was churning and I could feel my legs shaking. I tried to speak.***[7]** *My mouth felt like sandpaper.***[8]** *It was dry and rough and I couldn't form the words.*

87. Commas

1 and 2 Sentence A: Answer given on page 87. – They can comfort us in a crisis, help out when we're in trouble, **[comma needed here]**make us laugh or make us cry.
Sentence B: Correct
Sentence C: Correct
Sentence D: Answer given on page 87.
Sentence E: Correct
Sentence F: Incorrect – Although I had known her since primary school**, [comma needed here]**we never spoke again.
Sentence G: Incorrect – The problem**, [comma needed here]**which we may not want to face, is that friends can sometimes let us down.
Sentence H: Incorrect – A friend**, [comma needed here]**who I will not name**, [comma needed here]** once told me all my worst faults.
Sentence I: Correct

3 Answers will vary but all should aim to use commas correctly to separate:
- items in a list
- a main and subordinate clause
- a main and relative clause.

For example: When I think back, I know that Alice was the perfect friend. Funny, clever, unswervingly loyal and eminently talented, Alice was also one of the kindest people I have ever known. One day, I admired, with considerable feelings of envy, her violin. Without a moment of hesitation, Alice passed me the instrument, which was a valuable family heirloom, and encouraged me to try it out.

88. Apostrophes and speech punctuation

1 and 2 Sentence A: Incorrect – should be *don't*
Sentence B: Correct
Sentence C: Incorrect – should be *wouldn't*
Sentence D: Incorrect – should be *teacher's* because it is singular (one teacher)
Sentence E: Correct
Sentence F: Correct (plural: several boys' faces)
Sentence G: Correct
Sentence H: Correct
Sentence I: Incorrect – *'Come over here*, **[comma needed here]***' he whispered.*

3 Answers will vary but all should aim to use apostrophes and speech marks correctly. For example:
'Hey,' she called. 'Come over here.'
'What do you want?' I asked, **full of curiosity.**
'Have you heard about Adam?'
'No, nothing. What about him?'
'Keep your voice down!' she hissed, 'People will hear.'
'Hear what exactly?' I whispered, beginning to feel a little impatient.
'Well, you know what he's been like lately. Apparently, more than one teacher has phoned his parents to complain.'
'I'm not surprised,' I said, wondering what all the fuss was about.

89. Colons, semi-colons, dashes, brackets and ellipses

1 For example:
Sentence A – There is only one thing you can do to improve your grades: **[colon, followed by lower case r for revise]** revise.
Sentence B – Teachers can help: **[colon, followed by lower case t for they]** they can give revision tips and answer any questions you have about the exam.
Sentence C – Revision isn't easy: **[colon, followed by lower case i for it]** it takes time and willpower.
Sentence D – Exams are the problem; **[semi-colon, followed by lower case r for revision]** revision is the solution.

2 and 3 Sentence A: Correct
Sentence B: Correct
Sentence C: Incorrect – My bedroom walls are covered in scribbled revision notes and key points – not a pretty sight. (Brackets **must** be used in pairs; dashes can be used singly.)
Sentence D: Answer given on page 89.

4 Answers will vary but all should aim to use:
- a colon and a semi-colon
- dashes, brackets and an ellipsis.

For example: Deep breathing, positive mantras and assertive body language: this was Day One of the new me. I had never been a very confident person; I often struggled to believe in myself and in my own abilities. Yet, for a long time, it had been clear to me that something needed to change – and to change for the better. Many of my friends encouraged me, urging me on with warm words of support, while others (including my own mother) doubted I had the willpower to turn the corner. As I started to put the plans in place, I wondered who would turn out to be right …

90. Putting it into practice

Answers should feature a range of punctuation used accurately, including advanced punctuation such as colons and semi-colons.

91. Common spelling errors 1

1 A *their* (not *there*)
B *would have* (not *would of*); *absolutely* (not *absolutley*)
C *effect* (not *affect*); *extremely* (not *extremley*)
D Correct
E *There are* (not *Their our*)
F *They're* (not *There*)
G *its* (not *it's*)
H *definitely have* (not *definitley of*)
I *It's* (not *Its*); *are affected* (not *our effected*)
J *our* (not *are*)
K *could not have been* (not *could not of been*); *their* (not *there*)
L *negatively* (not *negativley*)
M *It's* (not *Its*)

92. Common spelling errors 2

1 A *where* (not *were*); *whose* (not *who's*)
B *Too* (not *To*)
C *passed* (not *past*)
D *pressure off us* (not *pressure of us*)
E *You're* (not *Your*)
F *Who's* (not *Whose*)
G *were* (not *where*)
H *past* (not *passed*); *were* (not *wear*)
I *to an extreme* (not *too an extreme*)
J Correct
K *you're* (not *your*)
L *off* (not *of*)
M *we're* (not *were*)

93. Common spelling errors 3

1 Correct spellings are:
argument
difficult
disappoint
disappear
embarrassing
possession
beginning
recommend
occasionally
definitely
separately
conscious
conscience
experience
independence
believe
weird
business
rhythm
decision
grateful

2 Spelling practised will vary.

94. Proofreading

1 The corrections needed in the extract are shown in **bold**.
Scotland is the most amazing place **I've** ever visite**d.** **Even** though it took ten hours to drive **there,** it was worth it the moment **I** saw **where** we were staying**: h**uge blue lochs, rolling green hills, miles and miles of pine forest. They even looked beautiful driving **past** them in **a** car.
On the first **day,** we took the dogs for a long walk through a forest**. It** was the quietest place **I've** ever been. Even with my brother **there**, all you could hear was the sound of **leaves** rustling in the breeze, the birds singing and **your** heart beating.
Our hotel was great**;** the **Scottish** people are so **friendly**. I would **definitely** stay there again.

2 Answers will vary depending on the work chosen.

3 Spelling practised will vary depending on the errors found for Question 2.

95. Putting it into practice

Answers should feature accurately used spelling, punctuation and grammar, and possibly signs of going back through the answer to make corrections.

For your own notes

For your own notes

For your own notes

For your own notes

For your own notes

Published by Pearson Education Limited, 80 Strand, London, WC2R 0RL.

www.pearsonschoolsandfecolleges.co.uk

Copies of official specifications for all Pearson qualifications may be found on the website: qualifications.pearson.com

Typeset by Tech-Set Ltd, Gateshead
Produced by Out of House Publishing

Illustrated by Tech-Set Ltd, Gateshead
Cover illustration by Miriam Sturdee

First published 2016

20 19 18 17
10 9 8 7 6 5

British Library Cataloguing in Publication Data
A catalogue record for this book is available from the British Library

ISBN 9781447987895

Printed in Slovakia by Neografia

Acknowledgements
The publisher would like to thank the following for their kind permission to reproduce their photographs:
123RF.com: 109c; **Fotolia.com:** 300dpi 109b; **Shutterstock.com:** Diego Cervo 106tr, Kekyalaynen 106tl, melissaf84 106br, simoly 106bl

All other images © Pearson Education

(Key: b-bottom; c-centre; l-left; r-right; t-top)

We are grateful to the following for permission to reproduce copyright material:
Extract on page 100 from 'Dear daughter' by Suzanne Whitton. Extract on page 101 from 'OK, you try teaching 13-year-olds', *The Guardian* (Hanson M) The Guardian; Extract on page 103 from ''Appy ever after', *The Sunday Times*, 30/11/2014 (Arlidge J) News UK; Extract on page 104 from *Unreliable Memoirs* by Clive James, reproduced with the permission of United Agents on behalf of Clive James; Extract on page 105 from *Bad Blood*, HarperCollins Publishers Ltd © (Lorna Sage, 2001); Extract on page 110–111 from *Oxford Observed: Town and Gown* by Peter Snow, John Murray (Peter Snow, 1992) reproduced with the permission of Peter Snow. Extract on page 103 from 'Turnaround in tourism as visitor numbers shoot up', The Oxford Mail, 24/08/2013 (Sophie Scott) Newsquest (Oxfordshire & Wiltshire) Ltd.

Note from the publisher
Pearson has robust editorial processes, including answer and fact checks, to ensure the accuracy of the content in this publication, and every effort is made to ensure this publication is free of errors. We are, however, only human, and occasionally errors do occur. Pearson is not liable for any misunderstandings that arise as a result of errors in this publication, but it is our priority to ensure that the content is accurate. If you spot an error, please do contact us at resourcescorrections@pearson.com so we can make sure it is corrected.